FOUNDATIONS *of* WORLD UNITY

FOUNDATIONS *of* WORLD UNITY

Compiled from
Addresses and Tablets
of

'ABDU'L-BAHÁ

"The gift of God to this enlightened age is
the knowledge of the oneness of mankind and of the fundamental
oneness of religion."

BAHÁ'Í PUBLISHING TRUST
WILMETTE, ILLINOIS

CONTENTS

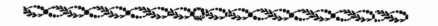

INTRODUCTION

THE search for a principle of unity capable of binding together the peoples of the world in some valid and creative relationship is undeniably the essential matter confronting the present generation. Nothing save world unity can release the vast productive energies at the disposal of the modern mind; nothing else can replace the racial idealisms which now, having served their day, become causes of conflict rather than sources of agreement; nothing short of this ultimate will stay the trends toward anarchy eating at the heart of the body politic in every organized nation. The swift, turbulent current of change runs too deep for any dam of compromise to restrain its power and effect some status of stability or repose behind which the human spirit may slumber beyond alarm. The very continuity of those myriad inter-relationships developed by competitive as well as cooperative forces depends upon the establishment of an organic unity corresponding to the inner not less than to the outer facts of life.

As the necessity for such a universal principle of unity appears more urgent and unescapable, humanity grows more sensitive to any influence capable of solving the continuous crisis which civilization has become.

The distinctive characteristic of the life-work of 'Abdu'l-Bahá consists in the fact that it was not merely a noble, self-sacrificing and tireless insistence upon world unity as an ideal, but likewise a definite presentation of world unity as a way of life. At a time when even the most enlightened liberalism conceived of unity in partial terms—a limited unity affecting only one plane of experience, such as religion, ethics, science or politics—'Abdu'l-Bahá by word and deed created a truly universal conception of the new term.

To 'Abdu'l-Bahá, world unity was not a mere linking together of formal institutions developed by society in its age of spiritual darkness and division, but a meeting and blending of minds and hearts awakened to a new consciousness of the destiny of humanity. As by the action of a pure solvent, his vision served to melt away the outer self imposed by environment and quicken the inmost center of being where response is to the universal Will. The purposes and powers of that Will were upheld by him in a victory of love so complete that the sum total of his life becomes a vindication not of a nation, not of a race, not of a religion, but of mankind.

But 'Abdu'l-Bahá stood as witness to the triumph of a love which is inseparable from mind. His interpretations of the fundamental human problems anticipated by a generation the conclusions of science and philosophy and possess a quality of synthesis which science and philosophy have never attained. The East and the West combined in his nature, preserving the integrity and essential truth of each type of experience; but his nature combined and reconciled also those humanly unrelated qualities of faith and reason, humanitarian love and justice, mystical devotion and administrative energy whose divergences in all men are the original cause of disunity in every form. His perception of the underlying oneness of life poured forth in an all-embracing sympathy and understanding the effect of which is like irrigation upon desert lands. Through this one life we have a glimpse of a united humanity in which universal attributes make possible new and superior social forms.

A superficial reading of his letters and public addresses, looking for the same treatment as would be given their topics by one confined to the established attitude of the religionist or social scientist, will fail utterly to make contact with the wisdom so freely offered the modern world in its hour of supreme need. This wisdom is revealed in statements compact with vision embracing a wider area of reality rather than in effort to develop any one thought or subject to its detailed fulness. His task did not include accomplishing any of the results of the specialist, but in re-establishing the wholeness of life.

A new mental and spiritual focus is required on the part of the reader himself; an attitude in which partisan victory or exclusive authority, subtle as well as gross, is less desirable than reality at any cost. When this focus is attained, assimilation of 'Abdu'l-Bahá's wisdom leads to a distinctive result, the gradual but certain relinquishment of those inner veils of prejudice which darken the understanding however active and keen the mind. For this wisdom is not the passive formula of the philosophic intellect, it is charged with an intensely energizing quality released from those depths where truth is lived as well as seen.

The present work consists of selections from public addresses delivered by 'Abdu'l-Bahá during his journey through Europe and America immediately preceding the War, or from letters written to friends in the West answering questions of similar theme. This journey was in itself a significant sign of world unity, in that he spoke before audiences representing practically every social division or interest of our complex modern life. From Columbia University in New York to Leland Stanford in California, from the Bowery Mission to the dinner table of a diplomat in Washington, 'Abdu'l-Bahá traversed not merely the geographical but also the spiritual area of the American people, leaving with them the assurance that if they can solve their greatest spiritual problem, amity and cooperation between the white and colored races, their influence will be decisive in promulgating universal peace.

In brief: 'Abdu'l-Bahá may be likened to a Rosetta stone inscribed with the human story in three languages—the language of the mind, the language of the heart, and the language of the spirit. By reference to this threefold reality, we find the key to that which is undeveloped in ourselves or unknown in the universe and thus approach that inner realization of God which is the foundation of the new age.

HORACE HOLLEY

Green Acre, Eliot, Maine
August 6, 1927

THE TRUE MODERNISM

ALL created things have their degree or stage of maturity. The period of maturity in the life of a tree is the time of its fruit-bearing. The maturity of a plant is the time of its blossoming and flower. The animal attains a stage of full growth and completeness, and in the human kingdom man reaches his maturity when the lights of intelligence have their greatest power and development.

From the beginning to the end of his life man passes through certain periods or stages each of which is marked by certain conditions peculiar to itself. For instance during the period of childhood his conditions and requirements are characteristic of that degree of intelligence and capacity. After a time he enters the period of youth in which his former conditions and needs are superseded by new requirements applicable to the advance in his degree. His faculties of observation are broadened and deepened, his intelligent capacities are trained and awakened, the limitations and environment of childhood no longer restrict his energies and accomplishments. At last he passes out of the period of youth and enters the stage or station of maturity which necessitates another transformation and corresponding advance in his sphere of life-activity. New powers and perceptions clothe him, teaching and training commensurate with his progression occupy his mind, special bounties and bestowals descend in proportion to his increased capacities and his former period of youth and its conditions will no longer satisfy his matured view and vision.

Similarly there are periods and stages in the life of the aggregate world of humanity which at one time was passing through its degree of childhood, at another its time of youth but now has entered its long presaged period of maturity, the evidences of which are everywhere visible and apparent. Therefore the requirements and conditions of former periods have changed and merged into exigencies which distinctly characterize the present age of the world of mankind. That which was applicable to human needs during the early history of the race could neither meet nor satisfy the demands of this day and period of newness and consummation. Humanity has emerged from its former degrees of limitation and preliminary training. Man must now become imbued with new virtues and powers, new moralities, new capacities. New bounties, bestowals and perfections are awaiting and already descending upon him. The gifts and graces of the period of youth although timely and sufficient during the adolescence of the world of mankind, are now incapable of meeting the requirements of its maturity. The playthings of childhood and infancy no longer satisfy or interest the adult mind.

From every standpoint the world of humanity is undergoing a re-formation. The laws of former governments and civilizations are in process of revision, scientific ideas and theories are developing and advancing to meet a new range of phenomena, invention and discovery are penetrating hitherto unknown fields revealing new wonders and hidden secrets of the material universe; industries have vastly wider scope and production; everywhere the world of mankind is in the throes of evolutionary activity indicating the passing of the old conditions and advent of the new age of re-formation. Old trees yield no fruitage; old ideas and methods are obsolete and worthless now. Old standards of ethics, moral codes and methods of living in the past will not suffice for the present age of advancement and progress.

This is the cycle of maturity and re-formation in religion as well. Dogmatic imitations of ancestral beliefs are passing. They have been the axis around which religion revolved but now are no longer fruitful; on the contrary, in this day they have become the cause of human degradation and hindrance. Bigotry and dogmatic adherence to ancient beliefs have become the central and fundamental source of animosity among men, the obstacle to human progress, the cause of warfare and strife, the destroyer of peace, composure and welfare in the world. Consider conditions in the Balkans today*; fathers, mothers, children in grief and lamentation, the foundations of life overturned, cities laid waste and fertile lands made desolate by the ravages of war. These conditions are the outcome of hostility and hatred between nations and peoples of religion who imitate and adhere to the forms and violate the spirit and reality of the divine teachings.

While this is true and apparent, it is likewise evident that the Lord of mankind has bestowed infinite bounties upon the world in this century of maturity and consummation. The ocean of divine mercy is surging, the vernal showers are descending, the Sun of Reality is shining gloriously. Heavenly teachings applicable to the advancement in human conditions have been revealed in this merciful age. This re-formation and renewal of the fundamental reality of religion constitute the true and outworking spirit of modernism, the unmistakable light of the world, the manifest effulgence of the Word of God, the divine remedy for all human ailment and the bounty of eternal life to all mankind.

---

* 1912.

THE SOURCE OF REALITY

IN our solar system, the center of illumination is the sun itself. Through the will of God this central luminary is the one source of the existence and development of all phenomenal things. When we observe the organisms of the material kingdoms we find that their growth and training are dependent upon the heat and light of the sun. Without this quickening impulse there would be no growth of tree or vegetation, neither would the existence of animal or human being be possible; in fact no forms of created life would be manifest upon the earth. But if we reflect deeply we will perceive that the great bestower and giver of life is God; the sun is the intermediary of His will and plan. Without the bounty of the sun therefore the world would be in darkness. All illumination of our planetary system proceeds or emanates from the solar center.

Likewise in the spiritual realm of intelligence and idealism there must be a center of illumination, and that center is the everlasting, ever-shining Sun, the Word of God. Its lights are the lights of reality which have shone upon humanity, illumining the realm of thought and morals, conferring the bounties of the divine world upon man. These lights are the cause of the education of souls and the source of the enlightenment of hearts, sending forth in effulgent radiance the message of the glad-tidings of the Kingdom of God. In brief, the moral and ethical world and the world of spiritual regeneration are dependent for their progressive being upon that heavenly center of illumination. It gives forth the light of religion and bestows the life of the spirit, imbues humanity with archetypal virtues and confers eternal splendors. This Sun of Reality, this center of effulgences is the prophet or Manifestation of God. Just as the phenomenal sun shines upon the material world producing life and growth, likewise the spiritual or prophetic Sun confers illumination upon the human world of thought and intelligence, and unless it rose upon the horizon of human existence the kingdom of man would become dark and extinguished.

The Sun of Reality is one Sun but it has different dawning-places, just as the phenomenal sun is one although it appears at various points of the horizon. During the time of spring the luminary of the physical world rises far to the north of the equinoctial; in summer it dawns midway and in winter it appears in the most southerly point of its zodiacal journey. These day-springs or dawning-points differ widely but the sun is ever the same sun whether it be the phenomenal or spiritual luminary. Souls who focus their vision upon the Sun of Reality will be the recipients of light no matter from what point it rises, but those who are fettered by adoration of the dawning-point are deprived when it appears in a different station upon the spiritual horizon.

Furthermore, just as the solar cycle has its four seasons, the cycle of the Sun of Reality has its distinct and successive periods. Each brings its vernal season or springtime. When the Sun of Reality returns to quicken the world of mankind a divine bounty descends from the heaven of generosity. The realm of thoughts and ideals is set in motion and blessed with new life. Minds are developed, hopes brighten, aspirations become spiritual, the virtues of the human world appear with freshened power of growth and the image and likeness of God become visible in man. It is the springtime of the inner world. After the spring, summer comes with its fullness and fruitage spiritual; autumn follows with its withering winds which chill the soul; the Sun seems to be going away until at last the mantle of winter overspreads and only faint traces of the effulgence of that divine Sun remain. Just as the surface of the material world becomes dark and dreary, the soil dormant, the trees naked and bare and no beauty or freshness remain to cheer the darkness and desolation, so the winter of the spiritual cycle witnesses the death and disappearance of divine growth and extinction of the light and love of God. But again the cycle begins and a new springtime appears. In it the former springtime has returned, the world is resuscitated, illumined and attains spirituality; religion is renewed and reorganized, hearts are turned to God, the summons of God is heard and life is again bestowed upon man. For a long time the religious world had been weakened and materialism had advanced; the spiritual forces of life were waning, moralities were becoming degraded, composure and peace had vanished from souls and satanic qualities were dominating hearts; strife and hatred overshadowed humanity, bloodshed and violence prevailed. God was neglected; the Sun of Reality seemed to have gone completely; deprivation of the bounties of heaven was a fact; and so the season of winter fell upon mankind. But in the generosity of God a new springtime dawned, the lights of God shone forth, the effulgent Sun of Reality returned and became manifest, the realm of thoughts and kingdom of hearts became exhilarated, a new spirit of life breathed into the body of the world and continuous advancement became apparent.

I hope that the lights of the Sun of Reality will illumine the whole world so that no strife and warfare, no battles and bloodshed remain. May fanaticism and religious bigotry be unknown, all humanity enter the bond of brotherhood, souls consort in perfect agreement, the nations of earth at last hoist the banner of truth and the religions of the world enter the divine temple of oneness, for the foundations of the heavenly religions are one reality. Reality is not divisible; it does not admit multiplicity. All the holy Manifestations of God have proclaimed and promulgated the same reality. They have summoned mankind to reality itself and reality is one. The clouds and mists of imitations have obscured the Sun of Truth. We must forsake these imitations, dispel these clouds and mists and free the Sun from the darkness of superstition. Then will the Sun of Truth shine most gloriously; then all the inhabitants of the world will be united, the religions will be one, sects and denominations will reconcile, all nationalities will flow together in the recognition of one fatherhood and all degrees of humankind gather in the shelter of the same tabernacle, under the same banner.

Until the heavenly civilization is founded, no result will be forthcoming from material civilization, even as you observe. See what catastrophes overwhelm mankind. Consider the wars which disturb the world. Consider the enmity and hatred. The existence of these wars and conditions indicates and proves that the heavenly civilization has not yet been established. If the civilization of the Kingdom be spread to all the nations, this dust of disagreement will be dispelled, these clouds will pass away and the Sun of Reality in its greatest effulgence and glory will shine upon mankind.

THE DAWN OF PEACE

THE fatherhood of God, His loving-kindness and beneficence are apparent to all. In His mercy he provides fully and amply for His creatures and if any soul sins He does not suspend His bounty. All created things are visible manifestations of His fatherhood, mercy and heavenly bestowals. Human brotherhood is likewise as clear and evident as the sun, for all are servants of one God, belong to one humankind, inhabit the same globe, are sheltered beneath the overshadowing dome of heaven and submerged in the sea of divine mercy. Human brotherhood and dependence exist because mutual helpfulness and cooperation are the two necessary principles underlying human welfare. This is the physical relationship of mankind. There is another brotherhood, the spiritual, which is higher, holier and superior to all others. It is heavenly; it emanates from the breaths of the Holy Spirit and the effulgence of merciful attributes; it is founded upon spiritual susceptibilities. This brotherhood is established by the Manifestations of the Holy One.

The divine Manifestations since the day of Adam have striven to unite humanity so that all may be accounted as one soul. The function and purpose of a shepherd is to gather and not disperse his flock. The prophets of God have been divine shepherds of humanity. They have established a bond of love and unity among mankind, made scattered peoples one nation and wandering tribes a mighty kingdom. They have laid the foundation of the oneness of God and summoned all to universal peace. All these holy, divine Manifestations are one. They have served one God, promulgated the same truth, founded the same institutions and reflected the same light. Their appearances have been successive and correlated; each one has announced and extolled the one who was to follow and all laid the foundation of reality. They summoned and invited the people to love and made the human world a mirror of the Word of God. Therefore the divine religions they established have one foundation; their teachings, proofs and evidences are one; in name and form they differ but in reality they agree and are the same. These holy Manifestations have been as the coming of springtime in the world. Although the springtime of this year is designated by another name according to the changing calendar, yet as regards its life and quickening it is the same as the springtime of last year. For each spring is the time of a new creation, the effects, bestowals, perfections and life-giving forces

14

of which are the same as those of the former vernal seasons although the names are many and various. This is 1912, last year's was 1911 and so on, but in fundamental reality no difference is apparent. The sun is one but the dawning-points of the sun are numerous and changing. The ocean is one body of water but different parts of it have particular designation, Atlantic, Pacific, Mediterranean, Antarctic, etc. If we consider the names, there is differentiation, but the water, the ocean itself is one reality.

Likewise the divine religions of the holy Manifestations of God are in reality one though in name and nomenclature they differ. Man must be a lover of the light no matter from what day-spring it may appear. He must be a lover of the rose no matter in what soil it may be growing. He must be a seeker of the truth no matter from what source it come. Attachment to the lantern is not loving the light. Attachment to the earth is not befitting but enjoyment of the rose which develops from the soil is worthy. Devotion to the tree is profitless but partaking of the fruit is beneficial. Luscious fruits no matter upon what tree they grow or where they may be found must be enjoyed. The word of truth no matter which tongue utters it must be sanctioned. Absolute verities no matter in what book they be recorded must be accepted. If we harbor prejudice it will be the cause of deprivation and ignorance. The strife between religions, nations and races arises from misunderstanding. If we investigate the religions to discover the principles underlying their foundations we will find they agree, for the fundamental reality of them is one and not multiple. By this means the religionists of the world will reach their point of unity and reconciliation. They will ascertain the truth that the purpose of religion is the acquisition of praiseworthy virtues, betterment of morals, spiritual development of mankind, the real life and divine bestowals. All the prophets have been the promoters of these principles; none of them has been the promoter of corruption, vice or evil. They have summoned mankind to all good. They have united people in the love of God, invited them to the religions of the unity of mankind and exhorted them to amity and agreement. For example, we mention Abraham and Moses. By this mention we do not mean the limitation implied in the mere names but intend the virtues which these names embody. When we say "Abraham" we mean thereby a Manifestation of divine guidance, a center of human virtues, a source of heavenly bestowals to mankind, a dawning-point of divine inspiration and perfections. These perfections and graces are not limited to names and boundaries. When we find these virtues, qualities and attributes in any personality, we recognize the same reality shining from within and bow in acknowledgment of the Abrahamic perfections. Similarly we acknowledge and adore the beauty of Moses. Some souls were lovers of the name Abraham, loving the lantern instead of the light and when they saw this same light shining from another lantern they were so attached to the former lantern that they did not recognize its later appearance and illumination. Therefore those who were attached and held tenaciously to the name Abraham were deprived when the Abrahamic virtues reappeared in Moses. Similarly the Jews were believers in His Holiness Moses, awaiting the coming of the Messiah. The virtues and perfections of Moses became apparent in His Holiness Jesus Christ most effulgently but the Jews held to the name Moses, not adoring the virtues and perfections manifest in him. Had they been adoring these virtues and seeking these perfections they would assuredly have believed in His Holiness Jesus Christ when the same virtues and perfections shone in him. If we are lovers of the light we adore it in whatever lamp it may become manifest but if we love the lamp itself and the light is transferred to another lamp we will neither accept nor sanction it. Therefore we must follow and adore the virtues revealed in the messengers of God whether in Abraham, Moses, Jesus or other prophets but we must not adhere to and adore the lamp. We must recognize the sun no matter from what dawning-point it may shine forth, be it Mosaic, Abrahamic or any personal point of orientation whatever, for we are lovers of sunlight and not of orientation. We are lovers of illumination and not of lamps and candles. We are seekers for water no matter from what rock it may gush forth. We are in need of fruit in whatsoever orchard it may be ripened. We long for rain it matters not which cloud pours it down. We must not be fettered. If we renounce these fetters we shall agree, for all are seekers of reality. The counterfeit or imitation of true religion has adulterated human belief and the foundations have been lost sight of. The variance of these imitations has produced enmity and strife, war and bloodshed. Now the glorious and brilliant twentieth century has dawned and the divine bounty is radiating universally. The Sun of Truth is shining forth in intense enkindlement. This is verily the century when these imitations must be forsaken, superstitions abandoned and God alone worshiped. We must look at the reality of the prophets and their teachings in order that we may agree.

Praise be to God! the springtime of God is at hand. This century is verily the spring season. The world of mind and the kingdom of soul have become fresh and verdant by its bestowals. It has resuscitated the whole realm of existence. On one hand the lights of reality are shining; on the other the clouds of divine mercy are pouring down the fullness of heavenly bounty. Wonderful material progress is evident and great spiritual discoveries are being made. Truly this can be called the miracle of centuries for it is replete with manifestations of the miraculous. The time has come when all mankind shall be united, when all races shall be loyal to one fatherland, all religions become one religion and racial and religious bias pass away. It is a day in which the oneness of humankind shall uplift its standard and international peace like the true morning flood the world with its light. Therefore we offer supplications to God, asking him to dispel these gloomy clouds and uproot these imitations in order that the East and West may become radiant with love and unity; that the nations of the world shall embrace each other and the ideal spiritual brotherhood illumine the world like the glorious sun of the high heavens.

THE CAUSE OF STRIFE

IN the estimation of historians this radiant century is equivalent to one hundred centuries of the past. If comparison be made with the sum total of all former human achievements it will be found that the discoveries, scientific advancement and material civilization of this present century have equaled, yea far exceeded the progress and outcome of one hundred former centuries. The production of books and compilations of literature alone bear witness that the output of the human mind in this century has been greater and more enlightening than all the past centuries together. It is evident therefore that this century is of paramount importance. Reflect upon the miracles of accomplishment which have already characterized it, the discoveries in every realm of human research, inventions, scientific knowledge, ethical reforms and regulations established for the welfare of humanity, mysteries of nature explored, invisible forces brought into visibility and subjection, a veritable wonder-world of new phenomena and conditions heretofore unknown to man now open to his uses and further investigation. The East and West can communicate instantly. A human being can soar in the skies or speed in submarine depths. The power of steam has linked the continents. Trains cross the deserts and pierce the barriers of mountains; ships find unerring pathways upon the trackless oceans. Day by day discoveries are increasing. What a wonderful century this is! It is an age of universal re-formation. Laws and statutes of governments civil and federal are in process of change and transformation. Sciences and arts are being moulded anew. Thoughts are metamorphosed. The foundations of human society are changing and strengthening. Today sciences of the past are useless. The ptolemaic system of astronomy, numberless other systems and theories of scientific and philosophical explanation are discarded, known to be false and worthless. Ethical precedents and principles cannot be applied to the needs of the modern world. Thoughts and theories of past ages are fruitless now. Thrones and governments are crumbling and falling. All conditions and requisites of the past unfitted and inadequate for the present time, are undergoing radical reform.

It is evident therefore that counterfeit and spurious religious teaching, antiquated forms of belief and ancestral imitations which are at variance with the foundations of divine reality must also pass away and be re-formed. They must be abandoned and new conditions be recognized. The morals of humanity must undergo change. New remedy and solution for human problems must be adopted. Human intellects themselves must change and be subject to the universal reformation. Just as the thoughts and hypotheses of past ages are fruitless today, likewise dogmas and codes of human invention are obsolete and barren of product in religion. Nay, it is true that they are the cause of enmity and conducive to strife in the world of humanity; war and bloodshed proceed from them and the oneness of mankind finds no recognition in their observance. Therefore it is our duty in this radiant century to investigate the essentials of divine religion, seek the realities underlying the oneness of the world of humanity and discover the source of fellowship and agreement which will unite mankind in the heavenly bond of love. This unity is the radiance of eternity, the divine spirituality, the effulgence of God and the bounty of the Kingdom. We must investigate the divine source of these heavenly bestowals and adhere unto them steadfastly. For if we remain fettered and restricted by human inventions and dogmas, day by day the world of mankind will be degraded, day by day warfare and strife will increase and satanic forces converge toward the destruction of the human race.

If love and agreement are manifest in a single family, that family will advance, become illumined and spiritual; but if enmity and hatred exist within it destruction and dispersion are inevitable. This is likewise true of a city. If those who dwell within it manifest a spirit of accord and fellowship it will progress steadily and human conditions become brighter whereas through enmity and strife it will be degraded and its inhabitants scattered. In the same way the people of a nation develop and advance toward civilization and enlightenment through love and accord, and are disintegrated by war and strife. Finally, this is true of humanity itself in the aggregate. When love is realized and the ideal spiritual bonds unite the hearts of men, the whole human race will be uplifted, the world will continually grow more spiritual and radiant and the happiness and tranquillity of mankind be immeasurably increased. Warfare and strife will be uprooted, disagreement and dissension pass away and universal peace unite the nations and peoples of the world. All mankind will dwell together as one family, blend as the waves of one sea, shine as stars of one firmament and appear as fruits of the same tree. This is the happiness and felicity of humankind. This is the illumination of man, the glory eternal and life everlasting; this is the divine bestowal. I desire this station for you and I pray God that the people of America may achieve this great end in order that the virtue of this democracy may be insured and their names be glorified eternally.

UNIVERSAL PEACE

TODAY there is no greater glory for man than that of service in the cause of the "Most Great Peace". Peace is light whereas war is darkness. Peace is life; war is death. Peace is guidance; war is error. Peace is the foundation of God; war is satanic institution. Peace is the illumination of the world of humanity; war is the destroyer of human foundations. When we consider outcomes in the world of existence we find that peace and fellowship are factors of upbuilding and betterment whereas war and strife are the causes of destruction and disintegration. All created things are expressions of the affinity and cohesion of elementary substances, and non-existence is the absence of their attraction and agreement. Various elements unite harmoniously in composition but when these elements become discordant, repelling each other, decomposition and non-existence result. Everything partakes of this nature and is subject to this principle, for the creative foundation in all its degrees and kingdoms is an expression or outcome of love. Consider the restlessness and agitation of the human world today because of war. Peace is health and construction; war is disease and dissolution. When the banner of truth is raised, peace becomes the cause of the welfare and advancement of the human world. In all cycles and ages war has been a factor of derangement and discomfort whereas peace and brotherhood have brought security and consideration of human interests. This distinction is especially pronounced in the present world conditions, for warfare in former centuries had not attained the degree of savagery and destructiveness which now characterizes it. If two nations were at war in olden times, ten or twenty thousand would be sacrificed but in this century the destruction of one hundred thousand lives in a day is quite possible. So perfected has the science of killing become and so efficient the means and instruments of its accomplishment that a whole nation can be obliterated in a short time. Therefore comparison with the methods and results of ancient warfare is out of the question.

According to an intrinsic law, all phenomena of being attain to a summit and degree of consummation, after which a new order and condition is established. As the instruments and science of war have reached the degree of thoroughness and proficiency, it is hoped that the transformation of the human world is at hand and that in the coming centuries all the energies and inventions of man will be utilized in promoting the interests of peace and brotherhood. Therefore may this esteemed and worthy society for the establishment of international peace* be confirmed in its sincere intentions and empowered by God. Then will it hasten the time when the banner of universal agreement will be raised and international welfare will be proclaimed and consummated so that the darkness which now encompasses the world shall pass away.

The powers of earth cannot withstand the privileges and bestowals which God has ordained for this great and glorious century. It is a need and exigency of the time. Man can withstand anything except that which is divinely intended and indicated for the age and its requirements. Now, Praise be to God! in all countries of the world, lovers of peace are to be found and these principles are being spread among mankind, especially in this country. Praise be to God! this thought is prevailing and souls are continually arising as defenders of the oneness of humanity, endeavoring to assist and establish international peace. There is no doubt that this wonderful democracy will be able to realize it and the banner of international agreement will be unfurled here to spread onward and outward among all the nations of the world. I give thanks to God that I find you imbued with such susceptibilities and lofty aspirations and I hope that you will be the means of spreading this light to all men. Thus may the Sun of Reality shine upon the East and West. The enveloping clouds shall pass away and the heat of the divine rays will dispel the mist. The reality of man shall develop and come forth as the image of God his creator. The thoughts of man shall take such upward flight that former accomplishments shall appear as the play of children;—for the ideas and beliefs of the past and the prejudices regarding race and religion have ever been lowering and destructive to human evolution. I am most hopeful that in this century these lofty thoughts shall be conducive to human welfare. Let this century be the sun of previous centuries the effulgences of which shall last forever, so that in times to come they shall glorify the twentieth century, saying the twentieth century was the century of lights, the twentieth century was the century of life, the twentieth century was the century of international peace, the twentieth century was the century of divine bestowals and the twentieth century has left traces which shall last forever.

* New York Peace Society.

THE PROPHETS AND WAR

WHEN we review history from the beginning down to the present day we find that strife and warfare have prevailed throughout the human world. Wars, religious, racial or political, have arisen from human ignorance, misunderstanding and lack of education. We will first consider religious strife and conflict.

It is evident that the divine prophets have appeared in the world to establish love and agreement among mankind. They have been the shepherds and not the wolves. The shepherd comes forth to gather and lead his flock and not to disperse them by creating strife. Every divine shepherd has assembled a flock which had formerly been scattered. Among the shepherds was His Holiness Moses. At a time when the tribes of Israel were wandering and dispersed, he assembled, united and educated them to higher degrees of capacity and progress until they passed out of the wilderness of discipline into the holy land of possession. He transformed their degradation into glory, changed their poverty into wealth and replaced their vices by virtues until they rose to such a zenith that the splendor of the sovereignty of Solomon was made possible and the fame of their civilization extended to the East and the West. It is evident therefore that His Holiness was a divine shepherd for he gathered the tribes of Israel together and united them in the power and strength of a great nationhood.

When the Messianic star of Jesus Christ dawned, he declared he had come to gather together the lost tribes or scattered sheep of Moses. He not only shepherded the flock of Israel, but brought together people of Chaldea, Egypt, Syria, ancient Assyria and Phoenicia. These people were in a state of utmost hostility, thirsting for the blood of each other with the ferocity of animals; but His Holiness Jesus Christ brought them together, cemented and united them in his cause and established such a bond of love among them that enmity and warfare were abandoned. It is evident therefore that the divine teachings are intended to create a bond of unity in the human world and establish the foundations of love and fellowship among mankind. Divine religion is not a cause for discord and disagreement. If religion becomes the source of antagonism and strife, the absence of religion is to be preferred. Religion is meant to be the quickening life of the body politic; if it be the cause of death to humanity, its nonexistence would be a blessing and benefit to man. Therefore in this

22

day the divine teachings must be sought, for they are the remedies for the present conditions of the world of humanity.

At a time when the Arabian tribes and nomadic peoples were widely separated, living in the deserts under lawless conditions, strife and bloodshed continual among them, no tribe free from the menace of attack and destruction by another,—at such a critical time Mohammed appeared. He gathered these wild tribes of the desert together, reconciled, united and caused them to agree so that enmity and warfare ceased. The Arabian nation immediately advanced until its dominion extended westward to Spain and Andalusia.

From these facts and premises we may conclude that the establishing of the divine religions is for peace, not for war and the shedding of blood. Inasmuch as all are founded upon one reality which is love and unity, the wars and dissensions which have characterized the history of religion have been due to imitations and superstitions which arise afterward. Religion is reality and reality is one. The fundamentals of the religion of God are therefore one in reality. There is neither difference nor change in the fundamentals. Variance is caused by blind imitations, prejudices and adherence to forms which appear later, and inasmuch as these differ, discord and strife result. If the religions of the world would forsake these causes of difficulty and seek the fundamentals, all would agree, and strife and dissension would pass away; for religion and reality are one and not multiple.

Other wars are caused by purely imaginary racial differences; for humanity is one kind, one race and progeny inhabiting the same globe. In the creative plan there is no racial distinction and separation such as Frenchman, Englishman, American, German, Italian or Spaniard; all belong to one household. These boundaries and distinctions are human and artificial, not natural and original. All mankind are the fruits of one tree, flowers of the same garden, waves of one sea. In the animal kingdom no such distinction and separation are observed. The sheep of the East and the sheep of the West would associate peacefully. The oriental flock would not look surprised as if saying, "These are sheep of the Occident; they do not belong to our country." All would gather in harmony and enjoy the same pasture without evidence of local or racial distinction. The birds of different countries mingle in friendliness. We find these virtues in the animal kingdom. Shall man deprive himself of these virtues? Man is endowed with superior reasoning power and the faculty of perception; he is the manifestation of divine bestowals. Shall racial ideas prevail and obscure the creative purpose of unity in his kingdom? Shall he say, "I am a German," "I am a Frenchman," or an "Englishman" and declare war because of this imaginary and human distinction? God forbid!

This earth is one household and the nativity of all humanity; therefore the human race should ignore distinctions and boundaries which are artificial and conducive to disagreement and hostility. We have come from the East. Praise be to God! we find this continent prosperous, the climate salubrious and delightful, the inhabitants genial and courteous, the government equable and just. Shall we entertain any other thought and feeling than that of love for you? Shall we say, "This is not our native land, therefore everything is objectionable?" This would be gross ignorance to which man must not subject himself. Man is endowed with powers to investigate reality, and the reality is that humanity is one in kind and equal in the creative plan. Therefore false distinctions of race and nativity which are factors and causes of warfare must be abandoned.

Consider what is happening* in Tripoli; how the poor are being killed and the blood of the helpless is being shed upon both sides; children made fatherless, fathers lamenting the death of their sons, mothers bewailing the loss of dear ones. And what is the benefit after all? Nothing conceivable. Is it therefore justifiable? The domestic animals do not manifest hatred and cruelty toward each other; that is the attribute of the wild and ferocious beasts. In a flock of one thousand sheep you will witness no bloodshed. Numberless species of birds are peaceful in flocks. Wolves, lions, tigers are ferocious because it is their natural and necessary means for obtaining food. Man has no need of such ferocity; his food is provided in other ways. Therefore it is evident that warfare, cruelty and bloodshed in the kingdom of man are caused by human greed, hatred and selfishness. The kings and rulers of nations enjoy luxury and ease in their palaces and send the common people to the battlefield; offer them as the food and targets of cannon. Each day they invent new instruments for the more complete destruction of the foundations of the human race. They are callous and merciless toward their fellow-creatures. What shall atone for the sufferings and grief of mothers who have so tenderly cared for their sons? What sleepless nights they have spent and what days of devotion and love they have given to bring their children to maturity! Yet the savagery of these warring rulers causes great numbers of their victims to be torn and mutilated in a day. What ignorance and degradation, yea even greater than the ferocious beasts themselves! For a wolf will carry away and devour one sheep at a time whereas an ambitious tyrant may cause the death of one hundred thousand men in a battle and glory in his military prowess saying, "I am commander-in-chief; I have won this mighty victory." Consider the ignorance and inconsistency of the human race. If a man kills another, no matter

---
*1912.

what the cause may be, he is pronounced a murderer, imprisoned or executed; but the brutal oppressor who has slain one hundred thousand is idolized as a hero, conqueror or military genius. A man steals a small sum of money; he is called a thief and sent to the penitentiary; but the military leader who invades and pillages a whole kingdom is acclaimed heroic and a mighty man of valor. How base and ignorant is man!

In Persia previous to the middle of the nineteenth century, among the various tribes and peoples, sects and denominations there existed the greatest animosity, strife and hatred. At that time too all the other nations of the East were in the same condition. Religionists were hostile and bigoted, sects were at enmity, races hated each other, tribes were constantly at war; everywhere antagonism and conflict prevailed. Men shunned and were suspicious of each other. The man who could kill a number of his fellow-creatures was glorified for his heroism and strength. Among religionists it was esteemed a praise-worthy deed to take the life of one who held an opposite belief. At this time Bahá'u'lláh arose and declared his mission. He founded the one-ness of the world of humanity, proclaimed that all are servants of the loving and merciful God who has created, nourished and provided for all, therefore why should men be unjust and unkind to each other, showing forth that which is contrary to God? As He loves us why should we entertain animosity and hate? If God did not love all He would not have created, trained and provided for all. Loving-kindness is the divine policy. Shall we consider human policy and attitude superior to the wisdom and policy of God? This would be inconceiv-able, impossible. Therefore we must emulate and follow the divine policy, dealing with each other in the utmost love and tenderness.

Bahá'u'lláh declared the "Most Great Peace" and international arbitration. He voiced these principles in numerous epistles which were circulated broadcast throughout the East. He wrote to all the kings and rulers encouraging, advising and admonishing them in regard to the establishment of peace; making it evident by conclusive proofs that the happiness and glory of humanity can only be assured through disarmament and arbitration. This was nearly fifty years ago. Because he promulgated the message of Universal Peace and interna-tional agreement, the kings of the Orient arose against him for they did not find their personal and national benefits advanced by his admonition and teaching. They persecuted him bitterly, inflicted upon him every torment, imprisoned, bastinadoed, banished him and eventually confined him in a fortress. Then they arose against his followers. For the establishment of international peace the blood of twenty thousand Bahá'ís was spilt. Their homes were destroyed, their children made captives and their possessions pillaged yet none of these people waxed cold or wavered in devotion. Even to this day the Bahá'ís are persecuted and quite recently a number were killed, for wherever they are found they put forth the greatest efforts to establish the peace of the world. They not only promulgate principles; they are people of action.

In Persia today through the teachings of Bahá'u'lláh you will find people of various religious beliefs and denominations living together in the utmost peace and agreement. The former enmities and hatred have passed away and they exercise the utmost love toward all mankind for they realize and know that all are the creatures and servants of one God. This is directly due to the divine teachings. At most it is simply this; that the ignorant must be educated, the ailing must be healed, those who are as children in the scale of development must be helped to reach the age of maturity. We must not be unfriendly to any one because of ignorance, neither must we reject the immature or turn away from the sick but administer the remedy for each human need until all are united in the providence of God. Therefore it is evident that the essential foundations of the divine religions are unity and love. If religion be productive of discord among mankind it is a destroyer and not divine for religion implies unity and binding together and not separation. Mere knowledge of principles is not sufficient. We all know and admit that justice is good but there is need of volition and action to carry out and manifest it. For example, we might think it good to build a church but simply thinking of it as a good thing will not help its erection. The ways and means must be provided; we must will to build it and then proceed with the construction. All of us know that international peace is good, that it is conducive to human welfare and the glory of man but volition and action are necessary before it can be established. Action is the essential. Inasmuch as this century is a century of light, capacity for action is assured to mankind. Necessarily the divine principles will be spread among men until the time of action arrives. Surely this has been so and truly the time and conditions are ripe for action now. All men know that verily war is a destroyer of human foundations and in every country of the world this is admitted and apparent. I find the United States of America an exceedingly progressive nation, the government just, the people in a state of readiness and the principle of equality established to an extraordinary degree. Therefore it is my hope that inasmuch as the standard of international peace must be upraised it may be upraised upon this continent, for this nation is more deserving and has greater capacity for such an initial step than any other. If other nations should attempt to do this the motive will be misunderstood. For instance, if Great Britain should declare for international peace it will be said that it has been done to insure the safety of her colonies. If France should hoist the standard other nations will declare some hidden diplomatic policy underlies the action; Russia would be suspected of national designs if the first step were taken by that people, and so on with all the European and eastern governments. But the United States of America could not be accused of any such selfish interest. Your government has, strictly speaking, no colonies to protect. You are not endeavoring to extend your domain nor have you need of territorial expansion. Therefore if America takes the first step toward the establishing of world peace it is certain to be ascribed to unselfishness and altruism. The world will say, "There is no other motive than altruism and service to humanity in this action by the United States." Therefore it is my hope that you may stand forth as the first herald of peace and hoist this banner; for this banner will be hoisted. Raise it aloft, for you are the most qualified and deserving of nations. The other countries await this summons, expect this call to the standard of reconciliation, for the whole world is distressed because of the excessive burden and irreparable damage of war. Taxes are levied to meet its drain. Every year the burden increases and the people have come to their end. Just now* Europe is a battlefield of ammunition ready for a spark; and one spark will set aflame the whole world. Before these complications and cataclysmic events happen, take the step to prevent it.

The foundations of all the divine religions are peace and agreement, but misunderstandings and ignorance have developed. If these are caused to disappear you will see that all the religious agencies will work for peace and promulgate the oneness of humankind. For the foundation of all is reality and reality is not multiple or divisible. His Holiness Moses founded it, His Holiness Jesus raised its tent, and its brilliant light has shone forth in all the religions. His Holiness Bahá'u'lláh proclaimed this one reality and spread the message of the "Most Great Peace". Even in prison he rested not until he lighted this lamp in the East. Praise be to God! all who have accepted his teachings are lovers of peace, peacemakers ready to sacrifice their lives and expend their possessions for it. Now let this standard be upraised in the West and many will respond to the call. America has become renowned for her discoveries, inventions and artistic skill, famous for equity of government and stupendous undertakings; now may she also become noted and celebrated as the herald and messenger of Universal Peace. Let this be her mission and undertaking and may its blessed impetus spread to all countries. I pray for all of you that you may render this service to the world of humanity.

*1912.

FOUNDATIONS OF WORLD UNITY

THERE is not one soul whose conscience does not testify that in this day there is no more important matter in the world than that of Universal Peace. Every just one bears witness to this and adores that esteemed Assembly* because its aim is that this darkness may be turned into light, this bloodthirstiness into kindness, this torment into bliss, this hardship into ease and this enmity and hatred into fellowship and love. Therefore the effort of those esteemed souls is worthy of praise and commendation.

But the wise souls who are aware of the essential relationships emanating from the realities of things consider that one single matter cannot, by itself, influence the human reality as it ought and should, for until the minds of men become united, no important matter can be accomplished. At present Universal Peace is a matter of great importance, but unity of conscience is essential, so that the foundation of this matter may become secure, its establishment firm and its edifice strong.

Therefore His Holiness Bahá'u'lláh fifty years ago, expounded this question of Universal Peace at a time when he was confined in the fortress of Akka and was wronged and imprisoned. He wrote about this matter of Universal Peace to all the great sovereigns of the world, and established it among his friends in the Orient. The horizon of the East was in utter darkness, nations displayed the utmost hatred and enmity towards each other, religions thirsted for each other's blood, and it was darkness upon darkness. At such a time His Holiness Bahá'u'lláh shone forth like the sun from the horizon of the East and illumined Persia with the light of these teachings.

Among his teachings was the declaration of Universal Peace. People of different nations, religions and sects, who followed him, came together to such an extent that remarkable gatherings were instituted, consisting of the various nations and religions of the East. Every soul who entered those gatherings saw but one nation, one pathway, one teaching, one order; for the teachings of His Holiness Bahá'u'lláh were not limited to the establishment of Universal Peace. They embraced many teachings which supplemented and supported that of Universal Peace.

Among these teachings is the independent investigation of reality,

---

*The members of the Central Organization for a Durable Peace, The Hague; to whom this Tablet was sent in reply to several letters.

so that the world of humanity might be saved from the darkness of imitation and attain to the truth; might tear off and cast away this ragged and outworn garment of one thousand years ago and put on the robe woven in the utmost purity and holiness in the loom of reality. As reality is one and cannot admit of multiplicity, therefore different opinions must ultimately become fused into one.

And among the teachings of His Holiness Bahá'u'lláh is the oneness of the world of humanity; that all human beings are the sheep of God and He is the kind Shepherd. This Shepherd is kind to all the sheep, because He created them all, trained them, provided for them and protected them. There is no doubt that the Shepherd is kind to all the sheep; and should there be among these sheep ignorant ones, they must be educated; if there be children, they must be trained until they reach maturity; if there be sick ones, they must be healed. There must be no hatred and enmity, for as by a kind physician these ignorant, sick ones should be treated.

And among the teachings of His Holiness Bahá'u'lláh is that religion must be the cause of fellowship and love. If it becomes the cause of estrangement, then it is not needed, for religion is like a remedy: if it aggravates the disease, then it becomes unnecessary.

And among the teachings of Bahá'u'lláh is that religious, racial, political, economic and patriotic prejudices destroy the edifice of humanity. As long as these prejudices prevail, the world of humanity will have no rest. For a period of six thousand years history informs us about the world of humanity. During these six thousand years the world of humanity has not been free from war, strife, murder and blood-thirstiness. In every period war has been waged in one country or another, and that war was due to either religious prejudice, racial prejudice, political prejudice or patriotic prejudice. It has, therefore, been ascertained and proved that all prejudices are destructive of the human edifice. As long as these prejudices persist, the struggle for existence must remain dominant, and bloodthirstiness and rapacity continue. Therefore, even as was the case in the past, the world of humanity cannot be saved from the darkness of nature, and cannot attain illumination, except through the abandonment of prejudices and the acquisition of the morals of the Kingdom. . . .

And among the teachings of His Holiness Bahá'u'lláh is the origination of one language that may be spread universally among the people. This teaching was revealed from the pen of Bahá'u'lláh in order that this universal language may eliminate misunderstandings from among mankind.

And among the teachings of His Holiness Bahá'u'lláh is the equality of women and men. The world of humanity has two wings—

one is woman and the other man. Not until both wings are equally developed can the bird fly. Should one wing remain weak, flight is impossible. Not until the world of woman becomes equal to the world of man in the acquisition of virtues and perfections, can success and prosperity be attained as they ought to be.

And among the teachings of Bahá'u'lláh is voluntary sharing of one's property with others among mankind. This voluntary sharing is greater than equality, and consists in this: that man should not prefer himself to others, but rather should sacrifice his life and property for others. But this should not be introduced by coercion so that it becomes a law and man is compelled to follow it. Nay, rather should man voluntarily and of his own choice sacrifice his property and life for others, and spend willingly for the poor, just as is done in Persia among the Bahá'ís.

And among the teachings of His Holiness Bahá'u'lláh is man's freedom: that through the Ideal Power he should be emancipated and free from the captivity of the world of nature; for as long as man is captive to nature he is a ferocious animal, as the struggle for existence is one of the exigencies of the world of nature. This matter of the struggle for existence is the fountain-head of all calamities, and is the supreme affliction.

And among the teachings of Bahá'u'lláh is that religion is a mighty bulwark. If the edifice of religion shakes and totters, commotion and chaos will ensue and the order of things will be utterly upset, for in the world of mankind there are two safeguards that protect man from wrongdoing. One is the law which punishes the criminal; but the law prevents only the manifest crime and not the concealed sin; whereas the ideal safeguard, namely, the religion of God, prevents both the manifest and the concealed crime, trains man, educates morals, compels the adoption of virtues and is the all-inclusive power which guarantees the felicity of the world of mankind. But by religion is meant that which is ascertained by investigation and not that which is based on mere imitation, the foundation of divine religions and not human imitations.

And among the teachings of Bahá'u'lláh is that although material civilization is one of the means for the progress of the world of mankind, yet until it becomes combined with divine civilization the desired result, which is the felicity of mankind, will not be attained. Consider! These battleships that reduce a city to ruins within the space of an hour are the result of material civilization; likewise the Krupp guns, the Mauser rifles, dynamite, submarines, torpedo boats, armed aircraft and bombing aeroplanes—all these weapons of war are malignant fruits of material civilization. Had material civilization been combined with divine civilization, these fiery weapons would never have been invented. Nay, rather human energy would have been wholly devoted to useful inventions and concentrated on praiseworthy discoveries. Material civilization is like a globe of glass. Divine civilization is the light itself, and the glass without the light is dark. Material civilization is like the body. No matter how infinitely graceful, elegant and beautiful it may be, it is dead. Divine civilization is like the spirit, and the body gets its life from the spirit, otherwise it becomes a corpse. It has thus been made evident that the world of mankind is in need of the breaths of the Holy Spirit. Without the spirit the world of mankind is lifeless, and without this light the world of mankind is in utter darkness. For the world of nature is an animal world. Until man is born again from the world of nature—that is to say, becomes detached from the world of nature, he is essentially an animal, and it is the teachings of God which convert this animal into a human soul.

And among the teachings of Bahá'u'lláh is the promotion of education. Every child must be instructed in sciences as much as is necessary. If the parents are able to provide the expenses of this education, it is all right; otherwise the community must provide the means for the teaching of that child.

And among the teachings of His Holiness Bahá'u'lláh are justice and right. Until these are realized on the plane of existence, all things will be in disorder and remain imperfect. The world of mankind is a world of oppression and cruelty, and a realm of aggression and error.

In fine, such teachings are numerous. These manifold principles, which constitute the greatest basis for the felicity of mankind and are of the bounties of the Merciful, must be added to the matter of Universal Peace and combined with it, so that results may accrue. Otherwise the realization of Universal Peace in the world of mankind is difficult. As the teachings of His Holiness Bahá'u'lláh are combined with Universal Peace, they are like a table provided with every kind of fresh and delicious food. Every soul can find at that table of infinite bounty that which he desires. If the question is restricted to Universal Peace alone, the remarkable results which are expected and desired will not be attained. The scope of Universal Peace must be such that all the communities and religions may find their highest wish realized in it. At present the teachings of His Holiness Bahá'u'lláh are such that all the communities of the world, whether religious, political or ethical, ancient or modern, find in the teachings of Bahá'u'lláh the expression of their highest wish.

For example, the people of religions find, in the teachings of His Holiness Bahá'u'lláh, the establishment of Universal Religion—a religion that perfectly conforms with present conditions, which in reality effects the immediate cure of the incurable disease, which relieves every pain and bestows the infallible antidote for every deadly poison. For if we wish to arrange and organize the world of mankind in accordance with the present religious imitations and thereby to establish the felicity of mankind, it is impossible and impracticable: for example, the enforcement of the laws of the Old Testament and also of the other religions in accordance with present imitations. But the essential basis of all the divine religions which pertains to the virtues of the world of mankind and is the foundation of the welfare of the world of man, is found in the teachings of His Holiness Bahá-'u'lláh in the most perfect presentation.

Similarly, with regard to the people who clamor for freedom: the moderate freedom which guarantees the welfare of the world of man, is found in the teachings of His Holiness Bahá'u'lláh.

So with regard to political parties: that which is the greatest policy directing the world of mankind, nay, rather the divine policy, is found in the teachings of His Holiness Bahá'u'lláh.

Likewise with regard to the party of "equality" which seeks the solution of the economic problems: until now all proposed solutions have proved impracticable except the economic proposals in the teachings of His Holiness Bahá'u'lláh, which are practicable and cause no distress to society.

So with the other parties: when ye look deeply into this matter, ye will discover that the highest aims of those parties are found in the teachings of Bahá'u'lláh. These teachings constitute the all-inclusive power among all men, and are practicable . . . .

For example, the question of Universal Peace, about which His Holiness Bahá'u'lláh says that the Supreme Tribunal must be established; although the League of Nations has been brought into existence, yet it is incapable of establishing Universal Peace. But the Supreme Tribunal which His Holiness Bahá'u'lláh has described will fulfill this sacred task with the utmost might and power. And his plan is this: that the national assemblies of each country and nation—that is to say, their parliaments—should elect two or three persons who are the choicest men of that nation, and are well informed concerning international laws and the relations between governments and aware of the essential needs of the world of humanity in this day. The number of these representatives should be in proportion to the number of inhabitants of that country. The election of these souls who are chosen by the national assembly—that is, the parliament—must be confirmed by the upper house, the congress and the cabinet and also by the president or monarch so that these persons may be the elected ones of all the nation and the government. From among these people the members of the Supreme Tribunal will be elected, and all mankind will thus have a share therein, for every one of these delegates is fully representative of his nation. When the Supreme Tribunal gives a ruling on any international question, either unanimously or by majority rule, there will no longer be any pretext for the plaintiff or ground of objection for the defendant. In case any of the governments or nations, in the execution of the irrefutable decision of the Supreme Tribunal, be negligent or dilatory, the rest of the nations will rise up against it, because all the governments and nations of the world are the supporters of this Supreme Tribunal. Consider what a firm foundation this is! But by a limited and restricted League the purpose will not be realized as it ought and should. This is the truth about the situation which has been stated. . . .

Today nothing but the power of the Word of God which encompasses the realities of things can bring the thoughts, minds, hearts and spirits under the shade of one Tree. He is the potent in all things, the vivifier of souls, the preserver and the controller of the world of mankind. Praise be to God, in this day the light of the Word of God has shone forth upon all regions; and from all sects, communities, nations, tribes, peoples, religions and denominations, souls have gathered together under the shadow of the Word of Oneness, and have in the utmost fellowship united and harmonized!

RACIAL HARMONY

TODAY I am most happy, for I see here* a gathering of the servants of God. I see the white and colored people together. In the estimation of God there is no distinction of color; all are one in the color and beauty of servitude to Him. Color is not important; the heart is all-important. It matters not what the exterior may be if the heart be pure and white within. God does not behold differences of hue and complexion; He looks at the hearts. He whose morals and virtues are praiseworthy is preferred in the presence of God; he who is devoted to the Kingdom is most beloved. In the realm of genesis and creation the question of color is of least importance.

The mineral kingdom abounds with many-colored substances and compositions but we find no strife among them on that account. In the kingdom of the plant and vegetable, distinct and variegated hues exist but the fruit and flowers are not in conflict for that reason. Nay, rather, the very fact that there is difference and variety lends a charm to the garden. If all were of the same color the effect would be monotonous and depressing. When you enter a rose-garden the wealth of color and variety of floral forms spread before you a picture of wonder and beauty. The world of humanity is like a garden and the various races are the flowers which constitute its adornment and decoration. In the animal kingdom also we find variety of color. See how the doves differ in beauty yet they live together in perfect peace, and love each other. They do not make difference of color a cause of discord and strife. They view each other as the same species and kind. They know they are one in kind. Often a white dove soars aloft with a black one. Throughout the animal kingdom we do not find the creatures separated because of color. They recognize unity of species and oneness of kind. If we do not find color distinction drawn in a kingdom of lower intelligence and reason, how can it be justified among human beings, especially when we know that all have come from the same source and belong to the same household? In origin and intention of creation mankind is one. Distinctions of race and color have arisen afterward.

Therefore today I am exceedingly glad that both white and colored people have gathered here and I hope the time will come when they shall live together in the utmost peace, unity and friendship. I wish to say one thing of importance to both in order that the white

*Howard University.

race may be just and kind to the colored and that the colored race may in turn be grateful and appreciative toward the white. The great proclamation of liberty and emancipation from slavery was made upon this continent. A long bloody war was fought by white men for the sake of colored people. These white men forfeited their possessions and sacrificed their lives by thousands in order that colored men might be freed from bondage. The colored population of the United States of America are possibly not fully informed of the wide-reaching effect of this freedom and emancipation upon their colored brethren in Asia and Africa where even more terrible conditions of slavery existed. Influenced and impelled by the example of the United States, the European powers proclaimed universal liberty to the colored race and slavery ceased to exist. This effort and accomplishment by the white nations should never be lost sight of. Both races should rejoice in gratitude, for the institution of liberty and equality here became the cause of liberating your fellow-beings elsewhere. The colored people of this country are especially fortunate, for, Praise be to God! conditions here are so much higher than in the East and comparatively few differences exist in the possibility of equal attainments with the white race. May both develop toward the highest degree of equality and altruism. May you be drawn together in friendship and may extraordinary development make brotherhood a reality and truth. I pray in your behalf that there shall be no name other than that of humanity among you.

Therefore strive earnestly and put forth your greatest endeavor toward the accomplishment of this fellowship and the cementing of this bond of brotherhood between you. Such an attainment is not possible without will and effort on the part of each; from one, expressions of gratitude and appreciation; from the other kindliness and recognition of equality. Each one should endeavor to develop and assist the other toward mutual advancement. This is possible only by conjoining of effort and inclination. Love and unity will be fostered between you, thereby bringing about the oneness of mankind. For the accomplishment of unity between the colored and whites will be an assurance of the world's peace. Then racial prejudice, national prejudice, limited patriotism and religious bias will pass away and remain no longer. I am pleased to see you at this gathering, white and dark, and I praise God that I have had this opportunity of seeing you loving each other, for this is the means of the glory of humanity. This is the means of the good-pleasure of God and of eternal bliss in His Kingdom. Therefore I pray in your behalf that you may attain to the fullest of love and that the day may come when all differences between you may disappear.

THE SPIRIT OF JUSTICE

WHAT could be better before God than thinking of the poor? For the poor are beloved by our heavenly Father. When His Holiness Christ came upon the earth those who believed in him and followed him were the poor and lowly, showing the poor were near to God. When a rich man believes and follows the Manifestation of God it is a proof that his wealth is not an obstacle and does not prevent him from attaining the pathway of salvation. After he has been tested and tried it will be seen whether his possessions are a hindrance in his religious life. But the poor are especially beloved of God. Their lives are full of difficulties, their trials continual, their hopes are in God alone. Therefore you must assist the poor as much as possible, even by sacrifice of yourself. No deed of man is greater before God than helping the poor. Spiritual conditions are not dependent upon the possession of worldly treasures or the absence of them. When physically destitute, spiritual thoughts are more likely. Poverty is stimulus toward God. Each one of you must have great consideration for the poor and render them assistance. Organize in an effort to help them and prevent increase of poverty. The greatest means for prevention is that whereby the laws of the community will be so framed and enacted that it will not be possible for a few to be millionaires and many destitute. One of Bahá'u'lláh's teachings is the adjustment of means of livelihood in human society. Under this adjustment there can be no extremes in human conditions as regards wealth and sustenance. For the community needs financier, farmer merchant and laborer just as an army must be composed of commander, officers and privates. All cannot be commanders; all cannot be officers or privates. Each in his station in the social fabric must be competent; each in his function according to ability; but justness of opportunity for all.

Lycurgus, king of Sparta, who lived long before the day of Christ, conceived the idea of absolute equality in government. He proclaimed laws by which all the people of Sparta were classified into certain divisions. Each division had its separate rights and function. First, farmers and tillers of the soil. Second, artisans and merchants. Third, leaders or grandees. Under the laws of Lycurgus the latter were not required to engage in any labor or vocation but it was incumbent upon them to defend the country in case of war and invasion. Then he divided Sparta into nine thousand equal parts or provinces, appoint-

36

ing nine thousand leaders or grandees to protect them. In this way the farmers of each province were assured of protection but each farmer was compelled to pay a tax to support the grandee of that province. The farmers and merchants were not obliged to defend the country. In lieu of labor the grandees received the taxes. Lycurgus in order to establish this forever as a law, brought nine thousand grandees together, told them he was going upon a long journey and wished this form of government to remain effective until his return. They swore an oath to protect and preserve his law. He then left his kingdom, went into voluntary exile and never came back. No man ever made such a sacrifice to insure equality among his fellowmen. A few years passed and the whole system of government he had founded collapsed, although established upon such a just and wise basis.

Difference of capacity in human individuals is fundamental. It is impossible for all to be alike, all to be equal, all to be wise. Bahá'u'lláh has revealed principles and laws which will accomplish the adjustment of varying human capacities. He has said that whatsoever is possible of accomplishment in human government will be effected through these principles. When the laws he has instituted are carried out there will be no millionaires possible in the community and likewise no extremely poor. This will be effected and regulated by adjusting the different degrees of human capacity. The fundamental basis of the community is agriculture, tillage of the soil. All must be producers. Each person in the community whose income is equal to his individual producing capacity shall be exempt from taxation. But if his income is greater than his needs he must pay a tax until an adjustment is effected. That is to say, a man's capacity for production and his needs will be equalized and reconciled through taxation. If his production exceeds he will pay no tax; if his necessities exceed his production he shall receive an amount sufficient to equalize or adjust. Therefore taxation will be proportionate to capacity and production and there will be no poor in the community.

COOPERATION

IT seems as though all creatures can exist singly and alone. For example, a tree can exist solitary and alone on a given prairie or in a valley or on the mountainside. An animal upon a mountain or a bird soaring in the air might live a solitary life. They are not in need of cooperation or solidarity. Such animated beings enjoy the greatest comfort and happiness in their respective solitary lives.

On the contrary, man cannot live singly and alone. He is in need of continuous cooperation and mutual help. For example, a man living alone in the wilderness will eventually starve. He can never, singly and alone, provide himself with all the necessities of existence. Therefore, he is in need of cooperation and reciprocity.

The mystery of this phenomenon, the cause thereof is this, that mankind has been created from one single origin, has branched off from one family. Thus in reality all mankind represents one family. God has not created any difference. He has created all as one that thus this family might live in perfect happiness and well-being.

Regarding reciprocity and cooperation: each member of the body politic should live in the utmost comfort and welfare because each individual member of humanity is a member of the body politic and if one member of the members be in distress or be afflicted with some disease all the other members must necessarily suffer. For example, a member of the human organism is the eye. If the eye should be affected that affliction would affect the whole nervous system. Hence, if a member of the body politic becomes afflicted, in reality, from the standpoint of sympathetic connection, all will share that affliction since this (one afflicted) is a member of the group of members, a part of the whole. Is it possible for one member or part to be in distress and the other members to be at ease? It is impossible! Hence God has desired that in the body politic of humanity each one shall enjoy perfect welfare and comfort.

Although the body politic is one family yet because of lack of harmonious relations some members are comfortable and some in direst misery, some members are satisfied and some are hungry, some members are clothed in most costly garments and some families are in need of food and shelter. Why? Because this family lacks the necessary reciprocity and symmetry. This household is not well arranged. This household is not living under a perfect law. All the laws which are legislated do not ensure happiness. They do not provide comfort.

Therefore a law must be given to this family by means of which all the members of this family will enjoy equal well-being and happiness.

Is it possible for one member of a family to be subjected to the utmost misery and to abject poverty and for the rest of the family to be comfortable? It is impossible unless those members of the family be senseless, atrophied, inhospitable, unkind. Then they would say, "Though these members do belong to our family—let them alone. Let us look after ourselves. Let them die. So long as I am comfortable, I am honored, I am happy—this my brother—let him die. If he be in misery let him remain in misery, so long as I am comfortable. If he is hungry let him remain so; I am satisfied. If he is without clothes, so long as I am clothed, let him remain as he is. If he is shelterless, home-less, so long as I have a home, let him remain in the wilderness."

Such utter indifference in the human family is due to lack of control, to lack of a working law, to lack of kindness in its midst. If kindness had been shown to the members of this family surely all the members thereof would have enjoyed comfort and happiness.

His Holiness Bahá'u'lláh has given instructions regarding every one of the questions confronting humanity. He has given teachings and instructions with regard to every one of the problems with which man struggles. Among them are (the teachings) concerning the question of economics that all the members of the body politic may enjoy through the working out of this solution the greatest happiness, welfare and comfort without any harm or injury attacking the general order of things. Thereby no difference or dissension will occur. No sedition or contention will take place. This solution is this:

First and foremost is the principle that to all the members of the body politic shall be given the greatest achievements of the world of humanity. Each one shall have the utmost welfare and well-being. To solve this problem we must begin with the farmer; there will we lay a foundation for system and order because the peasant class and the agricultural class exceed other classes in the importance of their service. In every village there must be established a general store-house which will have a number of revenues.

The first revenue will be that of the tenth or tithes.

The second revenue (will be derived) from the animals.

The third revenue, from the minerals, that is to say, every mine prospected or discovered, a third thereof will go to this vast store-house.

The fourth is this: whosoever dies without leaving any heirs all his heritage will go to the general storehouse.

Fifth, if any treasures shall be found on the land they should be devoted to this storehouse.

All these revenues will be assembled in this storehouse.

As to the first, the tenths or tithes: we will consider a farmer, one of the peasants. We will look into his income. We will find out, for instance, what is his annual revenue and also what are his expenditures. Now, if his income be equal to his expenditures, from such a farmer nothing whatever will be taken. That is, he will not be subjected to taxation of any sort, needing as he does all his income. Another farmer may have expenses running up to one thousand dollars we will say, and his income is two thousand dollars. From such an one a tenth will be required, because he has a surplus. But if his income be ten thousand dollars and his expenses one thousand dollars or his income twenty thousand dollars, he will have to pay as taxes, one-fourth. If his income be one hundred thousand dollars and his expenses five thousand, one-third will he have to pay because he has still a surplus since his expenses are five thousand and his income one hundred thousand. If he pays, say, thirty-five thousand dollars, in addition to the expenditure of five thousand he still has sixty thousand left. But if his expenses be ten thousand and his income two hundred thousand then he must give an even half because ninety thousand will be in that case the sum remaining. Such a scale as this will determine allotment of taxes. All the income from such revenues will go to this general storehouse.

Then there must be considered such emergencies as follows: a certain farmer whose expenses run up to ten thousand dollars and whose income is only five thousand, he will receive necessary expenses from the storehouse. Five thousand dollars will be allotted to him so he will not be in need.

Then the orphans will be looked after, all of whose expenses will be taken care of. The cripples in the village—all their expenses will be looked after. The poor in the village—their necessary expenses will be defrayed. And other members who for valid reasons are incapacitated—the blind, the old, the deaf—their comfort must be looked after. In the village no one will remain in need or in want. All will live in the utmost comfort and welfare. Yet no schism will assail the general order of the body politic.

Hence the expenses or expenditures of the general storehouse are now made clear and its activities made manifest. The income of this general storehouse has been shown. Certain trustees will be elected by the people in a given village to look after these transactions. The farmers will be taken care of and if after all these expenses are defrayed any surplus is found in the storehouse it must be transferred to the national treasury.

This system is all thus ordered so that in the village the very poor will be comfortable, the orphans will live happily and well; in a word, no one will be left destitute. All the individual members of the body politic will thus live comfortably and well.

For larger cities, naturally, there will be a system on a larger scale. Were I to go into that solution the details thereof would be very lengthy.

The result of this (system) will be that each individual member of the body politic will live most comfortably and happily under obligation to no one. Nevertheless, there will be preservation of degree because in the world of humanity there must needs be degrees. The body politic may well be likened to an army. In this army there must be a general, there must be a sergeant, there must be a marshal, there must be the infantry; but all must enjoy the greatest comfort and welfare.

God is not partial and is no respecter of persons. He has made provision for all. The harvest comes forth for everyone. The rain showers upon everybody and the heat of the sun is destined to warm everyone. The verdure of the earth is for everyone. Therefore there should be for all humanity the utmost happiness, the utmost comfort, the utmost well-being.

But if conditions are such that some are happy and comfortable and some in misery; some are accumulating exorbitant wealth and others are in dire want—under such a system it is impossible for man to be happy and impossible for him to win the good pleasure of God. God is kind to all. The good pleasure of God consists in the welfare of all the individual members of mankind.

A Persian king was one night in his palace, living in the greatest luxury and comfort. Through excessive joy and gladness he addressed a certain man, saying: "Of all my life this is the happiest moment. Praise be to God, from every point prosperity appears and fortune smiles! My treasury is full and the army is well taken care of. My palaces are many; my land unlimited; my family is well off; my honor and sovereignty are great. What more could I want!"

The poor man at the gate of his palace spoke out, saying: "O kind king! Assuming that you are from every point of view so happy, free from every worry and sadness—do you not worry for us? You say that on your own account you have no worries—but do you never worry about the poor in your land? Is it becoming or meet that you should be so well off and we in such dire want and need? In view of our needs and troubles how can you rest in your palace, how can you even say that you are free from worries and sorrows? As a ruler you must not be so egoistic as to think of yourself alone but you must think of those who are your subjects. When we are comfortable then you will be comfortable; when we are in misery how can you, as a king, be in happiness?"

The purport is this that we are all inhabiting one globe of earth. In reality we are one family and each one of us is a member of this family. We must all be in the greatest happiness and comfort, under a just rule and regulation which is according to the good pleasure of God, thus causing us to be happy, for this life is fleeting.

If man were to care for himself only he would be nothing but an animal for only the animals are thus egoistic. If you bring a thousand sheep to a well to kill nine hundred and ninety-nine the one remaining sheep would go on grazing, not thinking of the others and worrying not at all about the lost, never bothering that its own kind had passed away, or had perished or been killed. To look after one's self only is therefore an animal propensity. It is the animal propensity to live solitary and alone. It is the animal proclivity to look after one's own comfort. But man was created to be a man—to be fair, to be just, to be merciful, to be kind to all his species, never to be willing that he himself be well off while others are in misery and distress—this is an attribute of the animal and not of man. Nay, rather, man should be willing to accept hardships for himself in order that others may enjoy wealth; he should enjoy trouble for himself that others may enjoy happiness and well-being. This is the attribute of man. This is becoming of man. Otherwise man is not man—he is less than the animal.

The man who thinks only of himself and is thoughtless of others is undoubtedly inferior to the animal because the animal is not possessed of the reasoning faculty. The animal is excused; but in man there is reason, the faculty of justice, the faculty of mercifulness. Possessing all these faculties he must not leave them unused. He who is so hard-hearted as to think only of his own comfort, such an one will not be called man.

Man is he who forgets his own interests for the sake of others. His own comfort he forfeits for the well-being of all. Nay, rather, his own life must he be willing to forfeit for the life of mankind. Such a man is the honor of the world of humanity. Such a man is the glory of the world of mankind. Such a man is the one who wins eternal bliss. Such a man is near to the threshold of God. Such a man is the very manifestation of eternal happiness. Otherwise, men are like animals, exhibiting the same proclivities and propensities as the world of animals. What distinction is there? What prerogatives, what perfections? None whatever! Animals are better even—thinking only of themselves and negligent of the needs of others.

Consider how the greatest men in the world—whether among prophets or philosophers—all have forfeited their own comfort, have sacrificed their own pleasure for the well-being of humanity. They have sacrificed their own lives for the body politic. They have sacrificed their own wealth for that of the general welfare. They have forfeited their own honor for the honor of mankind. Therefore it becomes evident that this is the highest attainment for the world of humanity.

We ask God to endow human souls with justice so that they may be fair, and may strive to provide for the comfort of all, that each member of humanity may pass his life in the utmost comfort and welfare. Then this material world will become the very paradise of the Kingdom, this elemental earth will be in a heavenly state and all the servants of God will live in the utmost joy, happiness and gladness. We must all strive and concentrate all our thoughts in order that such happiness may accrue to the world of humanity.

The question of socialization is very important. It will not be solved by strikes for wages. All the governments of the world must be united and organize an assembly the members of which should be elected from the parliaments and the nobles of the nations. These must plan with utmost wisdom and power so that neither the capitalist suffer from enormous losses nor the laborers become needy. In the utmost moderation they should make the law; then announce to the public that the rights of the working people are to be strongly preserved. Also the rights of the capitalists are to be protected. When such a general plan is adopted by the will of both sides, should a strike occur, all the governments of the world collectively should resist it. Otherwise, the labor problem will lead to much destruction, especially in Europe. Terrible things will take place.

For instance, the owners of properties, mines and factories should share their incomes with their employees and give a fairly certain percentage of their products to their workingmen in order that the employees may receive, beside their wages, some of the general income of the factory so that the employee may strive with his soul in the work.

No more trusts will remain in the future. The question of the trusts will be wiped away entirely. Also, every factory that has ten thousand shares will give two thousand shares of these ten thousand to its employees and will write the shares in their names, so that they may have them, and the rest will belong to the capitalists. Then at the end of the month or year whatever they may earn after the expenses and wages are paid, according to the number of shares, should be divided among both. In reality, so far great injustice has befallen the common people. Laws must be made because it is impossible for the laborers to be satisfied with the present system. They will strike every month and every year. Finally, the capitalists will lose. In ancient times a strike occurred among the Turkish soldiers. They said to the government: "Our wages are very small and they should be increased." The government was forced to give them their demands. Shortly afterwards they struck again. Finally all the incomes went to the pockets of the soldiers to the extent that they killed the king, saying: "Why didst thou not increase the income so that we might have received more?"

It is impossible for a country to live properly without laws. To solve this problem rigorous laws must be made, so that all the governments of the world will be the protectors thereof.

In the Bolshevistic principles equality is effected through force. The masses who are opposed to the people of rank and to the wealthy class desire to partake of their advantages.

But in the divine teachings equality is brought about through a ready willingness to share. It is commanded as regards wealth that the rich among the people, and the aristocrats should, by their own free will and for the sake of their own happiness, concern themselves with and care for the poor. This equality is the result of the lofty characteristics and noble attributes of mankind.

THE CRITERIONS OF TRUTH

DURING my visit to London and Paris last year* I had many talks with the materialistic philosophers of Europe. The basis of all their conclusions is that the acquisition of knowledge of phenomena is according to a fixed, invariable law,—a law mathematically exact in its operation through the senses. For instance, the eye sees a chair; therefore there is no doubt of the chair's existence. The eye looks up into the heavens and beholds the sun; I see flowers upon this table; I smell their fragrance; I hear sounds outside, etc., etc. This, they say, is a fixed mathematical law of perception and deduction, the operation of which admits of no doubt whatever; for inasmuch as the universe is subject to our sensing, the proof is self-evident that our knowledge of it must be gained through the avenues of the senses. That is to say, the materialists announce that the criterion and standard of human knowledge is sense perception. Among the Greeks and Romans the criterion of knowledge was reason; that whatever is provable and acceptable by reason must necessarily be admitted as true. A third standard or criterion is the opinion held by theologians that traditions or prophetic statement and interpretations constitute the basis of human knowing. There is still another, a fourth criterion upheld by religionists and metaphysicians who say that the source and channel of all human penetration into the unknown is through inspiration. Briefly then, these four criterions according to the declarations of men are: First—Sense Perception; Second—Reason; Third—Traditions; Fourth—Inspiration.

In Europe I told the philosophers and scientists of materialism that the criterion of the senses is not reliable. For instance, consider a mirror and the images reflected in it. These images have no actual corporeal existence. Yet if you had never seen a mirror you would firmly insist and believe that they were real. The eye sees a mirage upon the desert as a lake of water but there is no reality in it. As we stand upon the deck of a steamer the shore appears to be moving, yet we know the land is stationary and we are moving. The earth was believed to be fixed and the sun revolving about it but although this appears to be so, the reverse is now known to be true. A whirling torch makes a circle of fire appear before the eye, yet we realize there is but one point of light. We behold a shadow moving upon the ground but

*1911.

it has no material existence, no substance. In deserts the atmospheric effects are particularly productive of illusions which deceive the eye. Once I saw a mirage in which a whole caravan appeared traveling upward into the sky. In the far north other deceptive phenomena appear and baffle human vision. Sometimes three or four suns called by scientists "mock suns" will be shining at the same time whereas we know the great solar orb is one and that it remains fixed and single. In brief, the senses are continually deceived and we are unable to separate that which is reality from that which is not.

As to the second criterion—reason—this likewise is unreliable and not to be depended upon. This human world is an ocean of varying opinions. If reason is the perfect standard and criterion of knowledge, why are opinions at variance and why do philosophers disagree so completely with each other? This is a clear proof that human reason is not to be relied upon as an infallible criterion. For instance, great discoveries and announcements of former centuries are continually upset and discarded by the wise men of today. Mathematicians, astronomers, chemical scientists continually disprove and reject the conclusions of the ancients; nothing is fixed, nothing final; everything continually changing because human reason is progressing along new roads of investigation and arriving at new conclusions every day. In the future much that is announced and accepted as true now will be rejected and disproved. And so it will continue ad infinitum.

When we consider the third criterion—traditions—upheld by theologians as the avenue and standard of knowledge, we find this source equally unreliable and unworthy of dependence. For religious traditions are the report and record of understanding and interpretation of the Book. By what means has this understanding, this interpretation been reached? By the analysis of human reason. When we read the Book of God the faculty of comprehension by which we form conclusions is reason. Reason is mind. If we are not endowed with perfect reason, how can we comprehend the meanings of the Word of God? Therefore human reason, as already pointed out, is by its very nature finite and faulty in conclusions. It cannot surround the Reality Itself, the Infinite Word. Inasmuch as the source of traditions and interpretations is human reason, and human reason is faulty, how can we depend upon its findings for real knowledge?

The fourth criterion I have named is inspiration through which it is claimed the reality of knowledge is attainable. What is inspiration? It is the influx of the human heart. But what are satanic promptings which afflict mankind? They are the influx of the heart also. How shall we differentiate between them? The question arises, How shall we know whether we are following inspiration from God or satanic promptings of the human soul? Briefly, the point is that in the human material world of phenomena these four are the only existing criterions or avenues of knowledge, and all of them are faulty and unrealiable. What then remains? How shall we attain the reality of knowledge? By the breaths and promptings of the Holy Spirit which is light and knowledge itself. Through it the human mind is quickened and fortified into true conclusions and perfect knowledge. This is conclusive argument showing that all available human criterions are erroneous and defective, but the divine standard of knowledge is infallible. Therefore man is not justified in saying "I know because I perceive through my senses"; or "I know because it is proved through my faculty of reason"; or "I know because it is according to tradition and interpretation of the holy book"; or "I know because I am inspired." All human standard of judgment is faulty, finite.

MAN AND NATURE

IF we look with a perceiving eye upon the world of creation, we find that all existing things may be classified as follows: First—Mineral—that is to say matter or substance appearing in various forms of composition. Second—Vegetable—possessing the virtues of the mineral plus the power of augmentation or growth, indicating a degree higher and more specialized than the mineral. Third—Animal—possessing the attributes of the mineral and vegetable plus the power of sense perception. Fourth—Human—the highest specialized organism of visible creation, embodying the qualities of the mineral, vegetable and animal plus an ideal endowment absolutely minus and absent in the lower kingdoms—the power of intellectual investigation into the mysteries of outer phenomena. The outcome of this intellectual endowment is science which is especially characteristic of man. This scientific power investigates and apprehends created objects and the laws surrounding them. It is the discoverer of the hidden and mysterious secrets of the material universe and is peculiar to man alone. The most noble and praiseworthy accomplishment of man therefore is scientific knowledge and attainment.

Science may be likened to a mirror wherein the images of the mysteries of outer phenomena are reflected. It brings forth and exhibits to us in the arena of knowledge all the product of the past. It links together past and present. The philosophical conclusions of bygone centuries, the teachings of the prophets and wisdom of former sages are crystallized and reproduced in the scientific advancement of today. Science is the discoverer of the past. From its premises of past and present we deduce conclusions as to the future. Science is the governor of nature and its mysteries, the one agency by which man explores the institutions of material creation. All created things are captives of nature and subject to its laws. They cannot transgress the control of these laws in one detail or particular. The infinite starry worlds and heavenly bodies are nature's obedient subjects. The earth and its myriad organisms, all minerals, plants and animals are thralls of its dominion. But man through the exercise of his scientific, intellectual power can rise out of this condition, can modify, change and control nature according to his own wishes and uses. Science, so to speak, is the "breaker" of the laws of nature.

Consider, for example, that man according to natural law should dwell upon the surface of the earth. By overcoming this law and restriction however he sails in ships over the ocean, mounts to the zenith in aeroplanes and sinks to the depths of the sea in submarines. This is against the fiat of nature and a violation of her sovereignty and dominion. Nature's laws and methods, the hidden secrets and mysteries of the universe, human inventions and discoveries, all our scientific acquisitions should naturally remain concealed and unknown, but man through his intellectual acumen searches them out of the plane of the invisible, draws them into the plane of the visible, exposes and explains them. For instance, one of the mysteries of nature is electricity. According to nature this force, this energy should remain latent and hidden, but man scientifically breaks through the very laws of nature, arrests it and even imprisons it for his use.

In brief, man through the possession of this ideal endowment of scientific investigation is the most noble product of creation, the governor of nature. He takes the sword from nature's hand and uses it upon nature's head. According to natural law, night is a period of darkness and obscurity, but man by utilizing the power of electricity, by wielding this electric sword overcomes the darkness and dispels the gloom. Man is superior to nature and makes nature do his bidding. Man is a sensitive being; nature is minus sensation. Man has memory and reason; nature lacks them. Man is nobler than nature. There are powers within him of which nature is devoid. It may be claimed that these powers are from nature itself and that man is a part of nature. In answer to this statement we will say that if nature is the whole and man is a part of that whole, how could it be possible for a part to possess qualities and virtues which are absent in the whole. Undoubtedly the part must be endowed with the same qualities and properties as the whole. For example, the hair is a part of the human anatomy. It cannot contain elements which are not found in other parts of the body, for in all cases the component elements of the body are the same. Therefore it is manifest and evident that man, although in body a part of nature, nevertheless in spirit possesses a power transcending nature; for if he were simply a part of nature and limited to material laws he could possess only the things which nature embodies. God has conferred upon and added to man a distinctive power, the faculty of intellectual investigation into the secrets of creation, the acquisition of higher knowledge, the greatest virtue of which is scientific enlightenment.

This endowment is the most praiseworthy power of man, for through its employment and exercise, the betterment of the human race is accomplished, the development of the virtues of mankind is made possible and the spirit and mysteries of God become manifest.

As material and physical sciences are taught here* and are con-

*Columbia University, New York City.

stantly unfolding in wider vistas of attainment, I am hopeful that spiritual development may also follow and keep pace with these outer advantages. As material knowledge is illuminating those within the walls of this great temple of learning, so also may the light of the spirit, the inner and divine light of the real philosophy glorify this institution. The most important principle of divine philosophy is the oneness of the world of humanity, the unity of mankind, the bond conjoining East and West, the tie of love which blends human hearts.

Therefore it is our duty to put forth our greatest efforts and summon all our energies in order that the bonds of unity and accord may be established among mankind. For thousands of years we have had bloodshed and strife. It is enough; it is sufficient. Now is the time to associate together in love and harmony. For thousands of years we have tried the sword and warfare; let mankind for a time at least live in peace. Review history and consider how much savagery, how much bloodshed and battle the world has witnessed. It has been either religious warfare, political warfare or some other clash of human interests. The world of humanity has never enjoyed the blessing of Universal Peace. Year by year the implements of warfare have been increased and perfected. Consider the wars of past centuries; only ten, fifteen or twenty thousand at the most were killed but now it is possible to kill one hundred thousand in a single day. In ancient times warfare was carried on with the sword; today it is the smokeless gun. Formerly battleships were sailing vessels; today they are dreadnoughts. Consider the increase and improvement in the weapons of war. God has created us all human and all countries of the world are parts of the same globe. We are all his servants. He is kind and just to all. Why should we be unkind and unjust to each other? He provides for all. Why should we deprive one another? He protects and preserves all. Why should we kill our fellow-creatures? If this warfare and strife be for the sake of religion, it is evident that it violates the spirit and basis of all religion. All the divine Manifestations have proclaimed the oneness of God and the unity of mankind. They have taught that men should love and mutually help each other in order that they might progress. Now if this conception of religion be true, its essential principle is the oneness of humanity. The fundamental truth of the Manifestations is peace. This underlies all religion, all justice. The divine purpose is that men should live in unity, concord and agreement and should love one another. Consider the virtues of the human world and realize that the oneness of humanity is the primary foundation of them all. Read the gospel and the other holy books. You will find their fundamentals are one and the same.

THE MICROCOSM AND THE MACROCOSM

WHEN we ponder over the reality of the microcosm, we discover that in the microcosm there are deposited three realities. Man is endowed with an outer or physical reality. It belongs to the material realm, the animal kingdom, because it has sprung from the material world. This animalistic reality of man he shares in common with the animals.

The human body is like animals subject to nature's laws. But man is endowed with a second reality, the rational or intellectual reality; and the intellectual reality of man predominates over nature.

All these sciences which we enjoy were the hidden and recondite secrets of nature, unknowable to nature, but man was enabled to discover these mysteries, and out of the plane of the unseen he brought them into the plane of the seen.

Yet there is a third reality in man, the spiritual reality. Through its medium one discovers spiritual revelations, a celestial faculty which is infinite as regards the intellectual as well as physical realms. That power is conferred upon man through the breath of the Holy Spirit. It is an eternal reality, an indestructible reality, a reality belonging to the divine, supernatural kingdom; a reality whereby the world is illumined, a reality which grants unto man eternal life. This third, spiritual reality it is which discovers past events and looks along the vistas of the future. It is the ray of the Sun of Reality. The spiritual world is enlightened through it, the whole of the Kingdom is being illumined by it. It enjoys the world of beatitude, a world which had not beginning and which shall have no end.

That celestial reality, the third reality of the microcosm, delivers man from the material world. Its power causes man to escape from nature's world. Escaping, he will find an illuminating reality, transcending the limited reality of man and causing him to attain to the infinitude of God, abstracting him from the world of superstitions and imaginations, and submerging him in the sea of the rays of the Sun of Reality.

This fact is proved from scientific as well as spiritual evidence.

When we ponder over the conditions of phenomena, we observe that all phenomena are composed of single elements. This singular cell-element travels and has its coursings through all the grades of existence. I wish you to ponder carefully over this. This cellular element has at some time been in the mineral kingdom. While staying in the mineral kingdom it has had its coursings and transformations through myriads of images and forms. Having perfected its journey in the mineral kingdom, it has ascended to the vegetable kingdom; and in the vegetable kingdom it has again had journeys and transformations through myriads of conditions. Having accomplished its functions in the vegetable kingdom, the cellular element ascends to the animal kingdom.

In the animal kingdom again it goes through the composition of myriads of images, and then we have it in the human kingdom. In the human kingdom likewise it has its transformations and coursings through multitudes of forms. In short, this single primordial atom has had its great journeys through every stage of life, and in every stage it was endowed with a special and particular virtue or characteristic.

Consequently, the great divine philosophers have had the following epigram: All things are involved in all things. For every single phenomenon has enjoyed the postulates of God, and in every form of these infinite electrons it has had its characteristics of perfection.

Thus this flower once upon a time was of the soil. The animal eats the flower or its fruit, and it thereby ascends to the animal kingdom. Man eats the meat of the animal, and there you have its ascent into the human kingdom, because all phenomena are divided into that which eats and that which is eaten. Therefore, every primordial atom of these atoms, singly and indivisible, has had its coursings throughout all the sentient creation, going constantly into the aggregation of the various elements. Hence do you have the conservation of energy and the infinity of phenomena, the indestructibility of phenomena, changeless and immutable, because life cannot suffer annihilation but only change.

The apparent annihilation is this: that the form, the outward image, goes through all these changes and transformations. Let us again take the example of this flower. The flower is indestructible. The only thing that we can see, this outer form, is indeed destroyed, but the elements, the indivisible elements which have gone into the composition of this flower are eternal and changeless. Therefore the realities of all phenomena are immutable. Extinction or mortality is nothing but the transformation of pictures and images, so to speak— the reality back of these images is eternal. And every reality of the realities is one of the bounties of God.

Some people believe that the divinity of God had a beginning. They say that before this particular beginning man had no knowledge of the divinity of God. With this principle they have limited the operation of the influences of God.

For example, they think there was a time when man did not exist, and that there will be a time in the future when man will not exist. Such a theory circumscribes the power of God, because how can we understand the divinity of God except through scientifically understanding the manifestations of the attributes of God?

How can we understand the nature of fire except from its heat, its light? Were not heat and light in this fire, naturally we could not say that the fire existed.

Thus, if there was a time when God did not manifest His qualities, then there was no God, because the attributes of God presuppose the creation of phenomena. For example, by present consideration we say that God is the *creator*. Then there must always have been a creation —since the quality of creator cannot be limited to the moment when some man or men realize this attribute. The attributes that we discover one by one—these attributes themselves necessarily anticipated our discovery of them. Therefore, God has no beginning and no ending; nor is His creation limited ever as to degree. Limitations of time and degree pertain to things created, never to the creation as a whole. They pertain to the forms of things, not to their realities. The effulgence of God cannot be suspended. The sovereignty of God cannot be interrupted.

As long as the sovereignty of God is immemorial, therefore the creation of our world throughout infinity is presupposed. When we look at the reality of this subject, we see that the bounties of God are infinite, without beginning and without end.

The greatest bounties of God in this phenomenal world are His Manifestations. This is the greatest postulate. These Manifestations are the Suns of Reality. For it is through the Manifestation that the *reality* becomes known and established for man. History proves to us that apart from the influence of the Manifestations, man sinks back into his animal condition, using even his intellectual power to subserve an animal purpose. Therefore there is no cessation whatsoever in the future for the appearance of the Manifestation of God, because God is infinite and His purpose cannot be limited in any way. If we ever dare to limit and circumscribe God's purpose within any bounds, then of necessity we have dared to set limitations to the omnipotence of God. The created has dared to define his Creator!

Consequently, the perfect man ever beholds the rays of the Sun of Truth. The perfect man ever awaits and expects the coming of the effulgence of God, he ever ponders over the methods and purposes of God, knowing that of certainty the realities of the Divine are not finite, the Divine names and attributes are not finite. God's graces and bounties are without limit, and the coming of the Manifestations of God are not circumscribed by time.

THE UNIVERSAL CYCLES

EACH one of the luminous bodies in this limitless firmament has a cycle of revolution which is of a different duration, and every one revolves in its own orbit, and again begins a new cycle. So the earth, every three hundred and sixty-five days, five hours, forty-eight minutes and a fraction, completes a revolution; and then it begins a new cycle, that is to say, the first cycle is again renewed. In the same way, for the whole universe, whether for the heavens or for men, there are cycles of great events, of important facts and occurrences. When a cycle is ended, a new cycle begins, and the old one, on account of the great events which take place, is completely forgotten, and not a trace or record of it will remain. As you see, we have no records of twenty thousand years ago, although we have before proved by argument that life on this earth is very ancient. It is not one hundred thousand, or two hundred thousand, or one million or two million years old; it is very ancient, and the ancient records and traces are entirely obliterated.

Each of the Divine Manifestations has likewise a cycle, and during the cycle his laws and commandments prevail and are performed. When his cycle is completed by the appearance of a new Manifestation, a new cycle begins. In this way cycles begin, end, and are renewed, until a universal cycle is completed in the world, when important events and great occurrences will take place which entirely efface every trace and every record of the past; then a new universal cycle begins in the world, for this universe has no beginning. We have before stated proofs and evidences concerning this subject; there is no need of repetition.

Briefly, we say a universal cycle in the world of existence signifies a long duration of time, and innumerable and incalculable periods and epochs. In such a cycle the Manifestations appear with splendor in the realm of the visible, until a great and universal Manifestation makes the world the center of his radiance. His appearance causes the world to attain to maturity, and the extension of his cycle is very great. Afterwards other Manifestations will arise under his shadow, who according to the needs of the time will renew certain commandments relating to material questions and affairs, while remaining under his shadow.

We are in the cycle which began with Adam, and its universal Manifestation is Bahá'u'lláh.

EDUCATION

ACCORDING to the statement of philosophers the difference in degree of humankind from lowest to highest is due to education. The proofs they advance are these: The civilization of Europe and America is an evidence and outcome of education whereas the semi-civilized and barbarous peoples of Africa bear witness in their condition that they have been deprived of its advantages. Education makes the ignorant wise, the tyrant just, promotes happiness, strengthens the mind, develops the will and makes fruitless trees of humanity fruitful. Therefore in the human world some have attained lofty degrees while others grope in the abyss of despair. Nevertheless the highest attainment is possible for every member of the human race even to the station of the prophets. This is the statement and reasoning of the philosophers.

The prophets of God are the first educators. They bestow universal education upon man and cause him to rise from lowest levels of savagery to the highest pinnacles of spiritual development. The philosophers too are educators along lines of intellectual training. At most they have only been able to educate themselves and a limited number about them, to improve their own morals and, so to speak, civilize themselves; but they have been incapable of universal education. They have failed to cause an advancement for any given nation from savagery to civilization.

It is evident that although education improves the morals of mankind, confers the advantages of civilization and elevates man from lowest degrees to the station of sublimity, there is nevertheless a difference in the intrinsic or natal capacity of individuals. Ten children of the same age, with equal station of birth, taught in the same school, partaking of the same food, in all respects subject to the same environment, their interests equal and in common, will evidence separate and distinct degrees of capability and advancement; some exceedingly intelligent and progressive, some of mediocre ability, others limited and incapable. One may become a learned professor while another under the same course of education proves dull and stupid. From all standpoints the opportunities have been equal but the results and outcomes vary from the highest to lowest degree of advancement. It is evident therefore that mankind differs in natal capacity and intrinsic intellectual endowment. Nevertheless although capacities are not the same, every member of the human race is capable of education.

His Holiness Jesus Christ was an educator of humanity. His teachings were altruistic; his bestowal universal. He taught mankind by the power of the Holy Spirit and not through human agency, for the human power is limited whereas the divine power is illimitable and infinite. The influence and accomplishment of Christ will attest this. Galen, the Greek physician and philosopher, who lived in the second century A. D., wrote a treatise upon the civilization of nations. He was not a Christian but he has borne testimony that religious beliefs exercise an extraordinary effect upon the problems of civilization. In substance he says,"There are certain people among us, followers of Jesus the Nazarene who was killed in Jerusalem. These people are truly imbued with moral principles which are the envy of philosophers. They believe in God and fear Him. They have hopes in His favors, therefore they shun all unworthy deeds and actions and incline to praiseworthy ethics and morals. Day and night they strive that their deeds may be commendable and that they may contribute to the welfare of humanity; therefore each one of them is virtually a philosopher, for these people have attained unto that which is the essence and purport of philosophy. These people have praiseworthy morals even though they may be illiterate."

The purpose of this is to show that the holy Manifestations of God, the divine prophets, are the first teachers of the human race. They are universal educators and the fundamental principles they have laid down are the causes and factors of the advancement of nations.

THE HOLY SPIRIT

THE elemental atoms which constitute all phenomenal existence and being in this illimitable universe are in perpetual motion, undergoing continuous degrees of progression. For instance, let us conceive of an atom in the mineral kingdom progressing upward to the kingdom of the vegetable by entering into the composition and fibre of a tree or plant. From thence it is assimilated and transferred into the kingdom of the animal and finally by the law and process of composition becomes a part of the body of man. That is to say, it has traversed the intermediate degrees and stations of phenomenal existence, entering into the composition of various organisms in its journey. This motion or transference is progressive and perpetual, for after disintegration of the human body into which it has entered, it returns to the mineral kingdom whence it came, and will continue to traverse the kingdoms of phenomena as before. This is an illustration designed to show that the constituent elemental atoms of phenomena undergo progressive transference and motion throughout the material kingdoms.

In its ceaseless progression and journeyings the atom becomes imbued with the virtues and powers of each degree or kingdom it traverses. In the degree of the mineral it possessed mineral affinities; in the kingdom of the vegetable it manifested the virtue augmentative or power of growth; in the animal organism it reflected the intelligence of that degree, and in the kingdom of man it was qualified with human attributes or virtues.

Furthermore, the forms and organisms of phenomenal being and existence in each of the kingdoms of the universe are myriad and numberless. The vegetable plane or kingdom for instance has its infinite variety of types and material structures of plant life, each distinct and different within itself, no two exactly alike in composition and detail, for there are no repetitions in nature, and the virtue augmentative cannot be confined to any given image or shape. Each leaf has its own particular identity, so to speak, its own individuality as a leaf. Therefore each atom of the innumerable elemental atoms, during its ceaseless motion through the kingdoms of existence as a constituent of organic composition, not only becomes imbued with the powers and virtues of the kingdoms it traverses but also reflects the attributes and qualities of the forms and organisms of those kingdoms. As each of these forms has its individual and particular virtue, therefore each elemental atom

57

of the universe has the opportunity of expressing an infinite variety of those individual virtues. No atom is bereft or deprived of this opportunity or right of expression. Nor can it be said of any given atom that it is denied equal opportunities with other atoms; nay, all are privileged to possess the virtues existent in these kingdoms and to reflect the attributes of their organisms. In the various transformations or passages from kingdom to kingdom, the virtues expressed by the atoms in each degree are peculiar to that degree. For example, in the world of the mineral, the atom does not express the vegetable form and organism, and when through the process of transmutation it assumes the virtues of the vegetable degree, it does not reflect the attributes of animal organisms, and so on.

It is evident then that each elemental atom of the universe is possessed of a capacity to express all the virtues of the universe. This is a subtle and abstract realization. Meditate upon it, for within it lies the true explanation of pantheism. From this point of view and perception, pantheism is a truth, for every atom in the universe possesses or reflects all the virtues of life, the manifestation of which is effected through change and transformation. Therefore the origin and outcome of phenomena is verily the omnipresent God for the reality of all phenomenal existence is through Him. There is neither reality nor the manifestation of reality without the instrumentality of God. Existence is realized and possible through the bounty of God, just as the ray or flame emanating from this lamp is realized through the bounty of the lamp from which it originates. Even so all phenomena are realized through the divine bounty, and the explanation of true pantheistic statement and principle is that the phenomena of the universe find realization through the one power animating and dominating all things; and all things are but manifestations of its energy and bounty. The virtue of being and existence is through no other agency. Therefore in the words of Bahá'u'lláh the first teaching is the oneness of the world of humanity.

Bahá'u'lláh has announced that no matter how far the world of humanity may advance in material civilization, it is nevertheless in need of spiritual virtues and the bounties of God. The spirit of man is not illumined and quickened through material sources. It is not resuscitated by investigating phenomena of the world of matter. The spirit of man is in need of the protection of the Holy Spirit. Just as he advances by progressive stages from the mere physical world of being into the intellectual realm, so must he develop upward in moral attributes and spiritual graces. In the process of this attainment he is ever in need of the bestowals of the Holy Spirit. Material development may be likened to the glass of a lamp whereas divine virtues and spiritual susceptibilities are the light within the glass. The lamp chimney is worthless without the light; likewise man in his material condition requires the radiance and vivification of the divine graces and merciful attributes. Without the presence of the Holy Spirit he is lifeless. Although physically and mentally alive he is spiritually dead. His Holiness Christ announced, "That which is born of flesh is flesh and that which is born of spirit is spirit," meaning that man must be born again. As the babe is born into the light of this physical world so must the physical and intellectual man be born into the light of the world of divinity. In the matrix of the mother the unborn child was deprived and unconscious of the world of material existence but after its birth it beheld the wonders and beauties of a new realm of life and being. In the world of the matrix it was utterly ignorant and unable to conceive of these new conditions but after its transformation it discovers the radiant sun, trees, flowers and an infinite range of blessings and bounties awaiting it. In the human plane and kingdom man is a captive of nature and ignorant of the divine world until born of the breaths of the Holy Spirit out of physical conditions of limitation and deprivation. Then he beholds the reality of the spiritual realm and kingdom, realizes the narrow restrictions of the mere human world of existence and becomes conscious of the unlimited and infinite glories of the world of God. Therefore no matter how man may advance upon the physical and intellectual plane he is ever in need of the boundless virtues of divinity, the protection of the Holy Spirit and the face of God.

SCIENCE

THE virtues of humanity are many but science is the most noble of them all. The distinction which man enjoys above and beyond the station of the animal is due to this paramount virtue. It is a bestowal of God; it is not material, it is divine. Science is an effulgence of the Sun of Reality, the power of investigating and discovering the verities of the universe, the means by which man finds a pathway to God. All the powers and attributes of man are human and hereditary in origin, outcomes of nature's processes, except the intellect, which is supernatural. Through intellectual and intelligent inquiry science is the discoverer of all things. It unites present and past, reveals the history of bygone nations and events, and confers upon man today the essence of all human knowledge and attainment throughout the ages. By intellectual processes and logical deductions of reason, this super-power in man can penetrate the mysteries of the future and anticipate its happenings.

Science is the first emanation from God toward man. All created beings embody the potentiality of material perfection, but the power of intellectual investigation and scientific acquisition is a higher virtue specialized to man alone. Other beings and organisms are deprived of this potentiality and attainment. God has created or deposited this love of reality in man. The development and progress of a nation is according to the measure and degree of that nation's scientific attainments. Through this means, its greatness is continually increased and day by day the welfare and prosperity of its people are assured.

All blessings are divine in origin but none can be compared with this power of intellectual investigation and research which is an eternal gift producing fruits of unending delight. Man is ever partaking of these fruits. All other blessings are temporary; this is an everlasting possession. Even sovereignty has its limitations and overthrow; this is a kingship and dominion which none may usurp or destroy. Briefly; it is an eternal blessing and divine bestowal, the supreme gift of God to man. Therefore you should put forward your most earnest efforts toward the acquisition of sciences and arts. The greater your attainment, the higher your standard in the divine purpose. The man of science is perceiving and endowed with vision whereas he who is ignorant and neglectful of this development is blind. The investigating mind is attentive, alive; the mind callous and indifferent is deaf and dead. A scientific man is a true index and representative of humanity, for through processes of inductive reasoning and research he is informed of all that appertains to humanity, its status, conditions and happenings. He studies the human body politic, understands social problems and weaves the web and texture of civilization. In fact, science may be likened to a mirror wherein the infinite forms and images of existing things are revealed and reflected. It is the very foundation of all individual and national development. Without this basis of investigation, development is impossible. Therefore seek with diligent endeavor the knowledge and attainment of all that lies within the power of this wonderful bestowal.

We have already stated that science or the attribute of scientific penetration is supernatural and that all other blessings of God are within the boundary of nature. What is the proof of this? All created things except man are captives of nature. The stars and suns swinging through infinite space, all earthly forms of life and existence whether mineral, vegetable or animal come under the dominion and control of natural law. Man through scientific knowledge and power rules nature and utilizes her laws to do his bidding. According to natural limitations he is a creature of earth restricted to life upon its surface, but through scientific utilization of material laws he soars in the sky, sails upon the ocean and dives beneath it. The products of his invention and discovery so familiar to us in daily life were once mysteries of nature. For instance, man has brought electricity out of the plane of the invisible into the plane of the visible, harnessed and imprisoned that mysterious natural agent and made it the servant of his needs and wishes. Similar instances are many but we will not prolong. Man as it were takes the sword out of nature's hand and with it for his sceptre of authority dominates nature itself. Nature is without the crown of human faculties and attributes. Man possesses conscious intelligence and reflection; nature is minus. This is an established fundamental among philosophers. Man is endowed with volition and memory; nature has neither. Man can seek out the mysteries latent in nature whereas nature is not conscious of her own hidden phenomena. Man is progressive; nature is stationary, without the power of progression or retrogression. Man is endowed with ideal virtues, for example intellection, volition,—among them faith, confession and acknowledgment of God, while nature is devoid of all these. The ideal faculties of man, including the capacity of scientific acquisition are beyond nature's ken. These are powers whereby man is differentiated and distinguished from all other forms of life. This is the bestowal of divine idealism, the crown adorning human heads. Nothwithstanding the gift of this supernatural power, it is most amazing that materialists still consider themselves within the bounds and captivity of nature. The truth is that God has endowed man with virtues, powers and ideal faculties of which nature is entirely bereft and by which man is elevated, distinguished and superior. We must thank God for these bestowals, for these powers He has given us, for this crown He has placed upon our heads.

How shall we utilize these gifts and expend these bounties? By directing our efforts toward the unification of the human race. We must use these powers in establishing the oneness of the world of humanity; appreciate these virtues by accomplishing the unity of the white and colored races; devote this divine intelligence to the perfecting of amity and accord among all branches of the human family, so that under the protection and providence of God, the East and West may hold each other's hands and become as lovers. Then will mankind be as one nation, one race and kind; as waves of one ocean. Although these waves may differ in form and shape, they are waves of the same sea. Flowers may be variegated in colors but they are all flowers of one garden. Trees differ though they grow in the same orchard. All are nourished and quickened into life by the bounty of the same rain; all grow and develop by the heat and light of the one sun; all are refreshed and exhilarated by the same breeze; that they may bring forth varied fruits. This is according to the creative wisdom. If all trees bore the same kind of fruit it would cease to be delicious. In their never ending variety man finds enjoyment instead of monotony.

And now as I look into your faces I am reminded of trees varying in color and form but all bearing luscious and delectable fruits, fragrant and delightful to the inner and outer senses. The radiance and spirituality of this meeting is through the favor of God. Our hearts are uplifted in thankfulness to Him. Praise be to God! you are living upon the great continent of the West enjoying the perfect liberty, security and peace of this just government. There is no cause for sorrow or unhappiness anywhere; every means of happiness and enjoyment is about you, for in this human world there is no greater blessing than liberty. You do not know. I who for forty years have been a prisoner, do know. I do know the value and blessing of liberty. For you have been and are now living in freedom and you have no fear of anybody. Is there a greater blessing than this? Freedom! Liberty! Security! These are the great bestowals of God. Therefore praise God!

SPIRITUAL SPRINGTIME

IN the world of existence man has traversed successive degrees
until he has attained the human kingdom. In each degree of his
progression he has developed capacity for advancement to the next
station and condition. While in the kingdom of the mineral he was attaining the capacity for promotion into the degree of the vegetable. In
the kingdom of the vegetable he underwent preparation for the world
of the animal and from thence he has come onward to the human degree or kingdom. Throughout this journey of progression he has ever
and always been potentially man.

In the beginning of his human life man was embryonic in the
world of the matrix. There he received capacity and endowment for
the reality of human existence. The forces and powers necessary for
this world were bestowed upon him in that limited condition. In this
world he needed eyes; he received them potentially in the other. He
needed ears; he obtained them there in readiness and preparation for
his new existence. The powers requisite in this world were conferred
upon him in the world of the matrix, so that when he entered this realm
of real existence he not only possessed all necessary functions and
powers but found provision for his material sustenance awaiting him.

Therefore in this world he must prepare himself for the life beyond. That which he needs in the world of the Kingdom must be
obtained here. Just as he prepared himself in the world of the matrix
by acquiring forces necessary in this sphere of existence, so likewise
the indispensable forces of the divine existence must be potentially
attained in this world.

What is he in need of in the Kingdom which transcends the life
and limitation of this mortal sphere? That world beyond is a world
of sanctity and radiance; therefore it is necessary that in this world
he should acquire these divine attributes. In that world there is need
of spirituality, faith, assurance, the knowledge and love of God. These
he must attain in this world so that after his ascension from the
earthly to the heavenly Kingdom he shall find all that is needful in
that life eternal ready for him.

That divine world is manifestly a world of lights; therefore man
has need of illumination here. That is a world of love; the love of God
is essential. It is a world of perfections; virtues or perfections must be
acquired. That world is vivified by the breaths of the Holy Spirit;

63

in this world we must seek them. That is the Kingdom of life everlasting; it must be attained during this vanishing existence.

By what means can man acquire these things? How shall he obtain these merciful gifts and powers? First, through the knowledge of God. Second, through the love of God. Third, through faith. Fourth, through philanthropic deeds. Fifth, through self-sacrifice. Sixth, through severance from this world. Seventh, through sanctity and holiness. Unless he acquires these forces and attains to these requirements he will surely be deprived of the life that is eternal. But if he possesses the knowledge of God, becomes ignited through the fire of the love of God, witnesses the great and mighty signs of the Kingdom, becomes the cause of love among mankind, and lives in the utmost state of sanctity and holiness, he shall surely attain to second birth, be baptized by the Holy Spirit and enjoy everlasting existence.

Is it not astonishing that although man has been created for the knowledge and love of God, for the virtues of the human world, for spirituality, heavenly illumination and life eternal, nevertheless he continues ignorant and negligent of all this? Consider how he seeks knowledge of everything except knowledge of God. For instance, his utmost desire is to penetrate the mysteries of the lowest strata of the earth. Day by day he strives to know what can be found ten metres below the surface, what he can discover within the stone, what he can learn by archaeological research in the dust. He puts forth arduous labors to fathom terrestrial mysteries but is not at all concerned about knowing the mysteries of the Kingdom, traversing the illimitable fields of the eternal world, becoming informed of the divine realities, discovering the secrets of God, attaining the knowledge of God, witnessing the splendors of the Sun of Truth and realizing the glories of everlasting life. He is unmindful and thoughtless of these. How much he is attracted to the mysteries of matter and how completely unaware he is of the mysteries of divinity! Nay, he is utterly negligent and oblivious of the secrets of divinity. How great his ignorance! How conducive to his degradation! It is as if a kind and loving father had provided a library of wonderful books for his son in order that he might be informed of the mysteries of creation; at the same time surrounding him with every means of comfort and enjoyment; but the son amuses himself with pebbles and playthings, neglectful of all his father's gifts and provision. How ignorant and heedless is man! The Father has willed for him glory eternal and he is content with blindness and deprivation. The Father has built for him a royal palace but he is playing with the dust; prepared for him garments of silk but he prefers to remain unclothed; provided for him delicious foods and fruits while he seeks sustenance in the grasses of the field.

Praise be to God! you have heard the call of the Kingdom. Your eyes are opened; you have turned to God. Your purpose is the good-pleasure of God, the understanding of the mysteries of the heart and investigation of the realities. Day and night you must strive that you may attain to the significances of the heavenly kingdom, perceive the signs of divinity, acquire certainty of knowledge and realize that this world has a creator, a vivifier, a provider, an architect,—knowing this through proofs and evidences and not through susceptibilities,—nay, rather, through decisive arguments and real vision; that is to say, visualizing it as clearly as the outer eye beholds the sun. In this way may you behold the presence of God and attain to the knowledge of the holy, divine Manifestations.

ETERNAL UNITY

WHAT is real unity? When we observe the human world we find various collective expressions of unity therein. For instance, man is distinguished from the animal by his degree or kingdom. This comprehensive distinction includes all the posterity of Adam and constitutes one great household or human family which may be considered the fundamental or physical unity of mankind. Furthermore, a distinction exists between various groups of humankind according to lineage, each group forming a racial unity separate from the others. There is also the unity of tongue among those who use the same language as a means of communication; national unity where various peoples live under one form of government such as French, German, British, etc.; and political unity which conserves the civil rights of parties or factions of the same government. All these unities are imaginary and without real foundation, for no real result proceeds from them. The purpose of true unity is real and divine outcomes. From these limited unities mentioned only limited outcomes proceed whereas unlimited unity produces unlimited result. For instance, from the limited unity of race or nationality the results at most are limited. It is like a family living alone and solitary; there are no unlimited or universal outcomes from it.

The unity which is productive of unlimited results is first a unity of mankind which recognizes that all are sheltered beneath the overshadowing glory of the All-Glorious; that all are servants of one God; for all breathe the same atmosphere, live upon the same earth, move beneath the same heavens, receive effulgence from the same sun and are under the protection of one God. This is the most great unity, and its results are lasting if humanity adheres to it; but mankind has hitherto violated it, adhering to sectarian or other limited unities such as racial, patriotic or unity of self-interests; therefore no great results have been forthcoming. Nevertheless it is certain that the radiance and favors of God are encompassing, minds have developed, perceptions have become acute, sciences and arts are widespread and capacity exists for the proclamation and promulgation of the real and ultimate unity of mankind which will bring forth marvelous results. It will reconcile all religions, make warring nations loving, cause hostile kings to become friendly and bring peace and happiness to the human world. It will cement together the Orient and Occident, remove forever the foundations of war and upraise the ensign of the "Most

Great Peace". These limited unities are therefore signs of that great unity which will make all the human family one by being productive of the attractions of conscience in mankind.

Another unity is the spiritual unity which emanates from the breaths of the Holy Spirit. This is greater than the unity of mankind. Human unity or solidarity may be likened to the body whereas unity from the breaths of the Holy Spirit is the spirit animating the body. This is a perfect unity. It creates such a condition in mankind that each one will make sacrifices for the other and the utmost desire will be to forfeit life and all that pertains to it in behalf of another's good. This is the unity which existed among the disciples of His Holiness Jesus Christ and bound together the prophets and holy souls of the past. It is the unity which through the influence of the divine spirit is permeating the Bahá'ís so that each offers his life for the other and strives with all sincerity to attain his good-pleasure. This is the unity which caused twenty thousand people in Persia to give their lives in love and devotion to it. It made the Bab the target of a thousand arrows and caused Bahá'u'lláh to suffer exile and imprisonment forty years. This unity is the very spirit of the body of the world. It is impossible for the body of the world to become quickened with life without its vivification. His Holiness Jesus Christ—may my life be a sacrifice to him!—promulgated this unity among mankind. Every soul who believed in Jesus Christ became revivified and resuscitated through this spirit, attained to the zenith of eternal glory, realized the life everlasting, experienced the second birth and rose to the acme of good fortune.

In the Word of God there is still another unity, the oneness of the Manifestations of God, His Holiness Abraham, Moses, Jesus Christ, Mohammed, the Bab and Bahá'u'lláh. This is a unity divine, heavenly, radiant, merciful; the one reality appearing in its successive manifestations. For instance, the sun is one and the same but its points of dawning are various. During the summer season it rises from the northern point of the ecliptic; in winter it appears from the southern point of rising. Each month between it appears from a certain zodiacal position. Although these dawning-points are different, the sun is the same sun which has appeared from them all. The significance is the reality of prophethood which is symbolized by the sun, and the holy Manifestations are the dawning-places or zodiacal points.

There is also the divine unity or entity which is sanctified above all concept of humanity. It cannot be comprehended nor conceived because it is infinite reality and cannot become finite. Human minds are incapable of surrounding that reality because all thoughts and conceptions of it are finite, intellectual creations and not the reality of divine being which alone knows itself. For example, if we form a conception of divinity as a living, almighty, self-subsisting, eternal being, this is only a concept apprehended by a human intellectual reality. It would not be the outward, visible reality which is beyond the power of human mind to conceive or encompass. We ourselves have an external, visible entity but even our concept of it is the product of our own brain and limited comprehension. The reality of divinity is sanctified above this degree of knowing and realization. It has ever been hidden and secluded in its own holiness and sanctity above our comprehending. Although it transcends our realization, its lights, bestowals, traces and virtues have become manifest in the realities of the prophets, even as the sun becomes resplendent in various mirrors. These holy realities are as reflectors, and the reality of divinity is as the sun which although it is reflected from the mirrors, and its virtues and perfections become resplendent therein, does not stoop from its own station of majesty and glory and seek abode in the mirrors; it remains in its heaven of sanctity. At most it is this, that its lights become manifest and evident in its mirrors or manifestations. Therefore its bounty proceeding from them is one bounty but the recipients of that bounty are many. This is the unity of God; this is oneness;—unity of divinity, holy above ascent or descent, embodiment, comprehension or idealization;—divine unity—the prophets are its mirrors; its lights are revealed through them; its virtues become resplendent in them, but the Sun of Reality never descends from its own highest point and station. This is unity, oneness, sanctity; this is glorification whereby we praise and adore God.

THE DARKENED LIGHTS

FROM the time of the creation of Adam to this day there have been two pathways in the world of humanity; one the natural or materialistic, the other the religious or spiritual. The pathway of nature is the pathway of the animal realm. The animal acts in accordance with the requirements of nature, follows its own instincts and desires. Whatever its impulses and proclivities may be it has the liberty to gratify them; yet it is a captive of nature. It cannot deviate in the least degree from the road nature has established. It is utterly minus spiritual susceptibilities, ignorant of divine religion and without knowledge of the Kingdom of God. The animal possesses no power of ideation or conscious intelligence; it is a captive of the senses and deprived of that which lies beyond them. It is subject to what the eye sees, the ear hears, the nostrils sense, the taste detects and touch reveals. These sensations are acceptable and sufficient for the animal. But that which is beyond the range of the senses, that realm of phenomena through which the conscious pathway to the Kingdom of God leads, the world of spiritual susceptibilities and divine religion,— of these the animal is completely unaware, for in its highest station it is a captive of nature.

One of the strangest things witnessed is that the materialists of today are proud of their natural instincts and bondage. They state that nothing is entitled to belief and acceptance except that which is sensible or tangible. By their own statements they are captives of nature, unconscious of the spiritual world, uninformed of the divine kingdom and unaware of heavenly bestowals. If this be a virtue the animal has attained it to a superlative degree, for the animal is absolutely ignorant of the realm of spirit and out of touch with the inner world of conscious realization. The animal would agree with the materialist in denying the existence of that which transcends the senses. If we admit that being limited to the plane of the senses is a virtue the animal is indeed more virtuous than man, for it is entirely bereft of that which lies beyond, absolutely oblivious of the Kingdom of God and its traces whereas God has deposited within the human creature an illimitable power by which he can rule the world of nature.

Consider how all other phenomenal existence and beings are captives of nature. The sun, that colossal center of our solar system, the giant stars and planets, the towering mountains, the earth itself and its kingdoms of life lower than the human,—all are captives of nature except man. No other created thing can deviate in the slightest degree from obedience to natural law. The sun in its glory and greatness millions of miles away is held prisoner in its orbit of universal revolution, captive of universal natural control. Man is the ruler of nature. According to natural law and limitation he should remain upon the earth, but behold how he violates this command and soars above the mountains in aeroplanes. He sails in ships upon the surface of the ocean and dives into its depths in submarines. Man makes nature his servant; harnesses the mighty energy of electricity for instance and imprisons it in a small lamp for his uses and conveniences. He speaks from the East to the West through a wire. He is able to store and preserve his voice in a phonograph. Though he is a dweller upon earth he penetrates the mysteries of starry worlds inconceivably distant. He discovers latent realities within the bosom of the earth, uncovers treasures, penetrates secrets and mysteries of the phenomenal world and brings to light that which according to nature's jealous laws should remain hidden, unknown and unfathomable. Through an ideal inner power man brings these realities forth from the invisible plane to the visible. This is contrary to nature's law.

It is evident therefore that man is ruler over nature's sphere and province. Nature is inert, man is progressive. Nature has no consciousness, man is endowed with it. Nature is without volition and acts perforce whereas man possesses a mighty will. Nature is incapable of discovering mysteries or realities whereas man is especially fitted to do so. Nature is not in touch with the realm of God, man is attuned to its evidences. Nature is uninformed of God, man is conscious of Him. Man acquires divine virtues, nature is denied them. Man can voluntarily discontinue vices, nature has no power to modify the influence of its instincts. Altogether it is evident that man is more noble and superior; that in him there is an ideal power surpassing nature. He has consciousness, volition, memory, intelligent power, divine attributes and virtues of which nature is completely deprived, bereft and minus; therefore man is higher and nobler by reason of the ideal and heavenly force latent and manifest in him.

How strange then it seems that man, notwithstanding his endowment with this ideal power, will descend to a level beneath him and declare himself no greater than that which is manifestly inferior to his real station. God has created such a conscious spirit within him that he is the most wonderful of all contingent beings. In ignoring these virtues he descends to the material plane, considers matter the ruler of existence and denies that which lies beyond. Is this virtue? In its fullest sense this is animalistic, for the animal realizes nothing more. In fact from this standpoint the animal is the greater philosopher because it is completely ignorant of the Kingdom of God, possesses no spiritual susceptibilities and is uninformed of the heavenly world. In brief, this is a view of the pathway of nature.

The second pathway is that of religion, the road of the divine Kingdom. It involves the acquisition of praiseworthy attributes, heavenly illumination and righteous actions in the world of humanity. This pathway is conducive to the progress and uplift of the world. It is the source of human enlightenment, training and ethical improvement; the magnet which attracts the love of God because of the knowledge of God it bestows. This is the road of the holy Manifestations of God for they are in reality the foundation of the divine religion of oneness. There is no change or transformation in this pathway. It is the cause of human betterment, the acquisition of heavenly virtues and the illumination of mankind.

Alas! that humanity is completely submerged in imitations and unrealities notwithstanding the truth of divine religion has ever remained the same. Superstitions have obscured the fundamental reality, the world is darkened and the light of religion is not apparent. This darkness is conducive to differences and dissensions; rites and dogmas are many and various; therefore discord has arisen among the religious systems whereas religion is for the unification of mankind. True religion is the source of love and agreement amongst men, the cause of the development of praiseworthy qualities; but the people are holding to the counterfeit and imitation, negligent of the reality which unifies; so they are bereft and deprived of the radiance of religion. They follow superstitions inherited from their fathers and ancestors. To such an extent has this prevailed that they have taken away the heavenly light of divine truth and sit in the darkness of imitations and imaginations. That which was meant to be conducive to life has become the cause of death; that which should have been an evidence of knowledge is now a proof of ignorance; that which was a factor in the sublimity of human nature has proved to be its degradation. Therefore the realm of the religionist has gradually narrowed and darkened and the sphere of the materialist has widened and advanced; for the religionist has held to imitation and counterfeit, neglecting and discarding holiness and the sacred reality of religion. When the sun sets it is the time for bats to fly. They come forth because they are creatures of the night. When the lights of religion become darkened the materialists appear. They are the bats of night. The decline of religion is their time of activity; they seek the shadows when the world is darkened and clouds have spread over it.

THE NEED OF DIVINE EDUCATION

IN the books of the prophets certain glad-tidings are recorded which are absolutely true and free from doubt. The East has ever been the dawning-point of the Sun of Reality. All the prophets of God have appeared there. The religions of God have been promulgated, the teachings of God have been spread and the law of God founded in the East. The Orient has always been the center of lights. The West has acquired illumination from the East but in some respects the reflection of the light has been greater in the Occident. This is especially true of Christianity. His Holiness Christ appeared in Palestine and his teachings were founded there. Although the doors of the Kingdom were opened in that country and the bestowals of divinity were spread broadcast from its center, the people of the West have embraced and promulgated Christianity more fully than those in the East. The Sun of Reality shone forth from the horizon of the East but its heat and ray are most resplendent in the West where the radiant standard of His Holiness Christ has been upraised. I have great hopes that the lights of Bahá'u'lláh's appearance may also find the fullest manifestation and reflection in these western regions; for the teachings of Bahá'u'lláh are especially applicable to the conditions of the people here. The western nations are endowed with the capability of understanding the rational and peerless words of Bahá'u'lláh and realizing that the essence of the teachings of all the former prophets can be found in his utterance.

The teachings of His Holiness Christ have been promulgated by His Holiness Bahá'u'lláh who has also revealed new teachings applicable to present conditions in the world of humanity. He has trained the people of the East through the power and protection of the Holy Spirit, cemented the souls of humanity together and established the foundations of international unity.

Through the power of his words the hearts of the people of all religions have been attuned in harmony. For instance, among the Bahá'ís in Persia there are Christians, Mohammedans, Zoroastrians, Jews and many others of varying denominations and beliefs who have been brought together in unity and love in the cause of Bahá'u'lláh. Although these people were formerly hostile and antagonistic, filled with hatred and bitterness toward each other, blood-thirsty and pillaging, considering that animosity and attack were the means of attaining the good-pleasure of God, they have now become loving

72

and filled with the radiant zeal of fellowship and brotherhood, the purpose of them all being service to the world of humanity, promotion of international peace, the unification of the divine religions and deeds of universal philanthropy. By their words and actions they are proving the verity of His Holiness Bahá'u'lláh.

Consider the animosity and hatred existing today between the various nations of the world. What disagreements and hostilities arise, what warfare and contention, how much bloodshed, what injustice and tyranny! Just now there is war in eastern Turkey, also war between Turkey and Italy. Nations are devoted to conquest and bloodshed, filled with the animus of religious hatred, seeking the good-pleasure of God by killing and destroying those whom they consider enemies in their blindness. How ignorant they are! That which is forbidden by God they consider acceptable to Him. God is love; God seeketh fellowship, purity, sanctity and long-suffering; these are the attributes of divinity. Therefore these warring, raging nations have arisen against divinity, imagining they are serving God. What gross ignorance this is! What injustice, blindness and lack of realization! Briefly; we must strive with heart and soul in order that this darkness of the contingent world may be dispelled, that the lights of the Kingdom shall shine upon all the horizons, the world of humanity become illumined, the image of God become apparent in human mirrors, the law of God be well established and that all regions of the world shall enjoy peace, comfort and composure beneath the equitable protection of God. My admonition and exhortation to you is this: Be kind to all people, love humanity, consider all mankind as your relations and servants of the most high God. Strive day and night that animosity and contention may pass away from the hearts of men, that all religions shall become reconciled and the nations love each other, so that no racial, religious or political prejudice may remain and the world of humanity behold God as the beginning and end of all existence. God has created all and all return to God. Therefore love humanity with all your heart and soul. If you meet a poor man, assist him; if you see the sick, heal him; reassure the affrighted one, render the cowardly noble and courageous, educate the ignorant, associate with the stranger. Emulate God. Consider how kindly, how lovingly He deals with all and follow His example. You must treat people in accordance with the divine precepts; in other words, treat them as kindly as God treats them, for this is the greatest attainment possible for the world of humanity.

Furthermore, know ye that God has created in man the power of reason whereby man is enabled to investigate reality. God has not intended man to blindly imitate his fathers and ancestors. He has endowed him with mind or the faculty of reasoning by the exercise of which he is to investigate and discover the truth; and that which he finds real and true, he must accept. He must not be an imitator or blind follower of any soul. He must not rely implicitly upon the opinion of any man without investigation; nay, each soul must seek intelligently and independently, arriving at a real conclusion and bound only by that reality. The greatest cause of bereavement and disheartening in the world of humanity is ignorance based upon blind imitation. It is due to this that wars and battles prevail; from this cause hatred and animosity arise continually among mankind. Through failure to investigate reality the Jews rejected His Holiness Jesus Christ. They were expecting his coming; by day and night they mourned and lamented, saying, "O God! hasten thou the day of the advent of Christ," expressing most intense longing for the Messiah but when His Holiness Christ appeared they denied and rejected him, treated him with arrogant contempt, sentenced him to death and finally crucified him. Why did this happen? Because they were blindly following imitations, believing that which had descended to them as a heritage from their fathers and ancestors; tenaciously holding to it and refusing to investigate the reality of Christ. Therefore they were deprived of the bounties of His Holiness whereas if they had forsaken imitations and investigated the reality of the Messiah they would have surely been guided to believing in him. Instead of this, they said, "We have heard from our fathers and have read in the old testament that His Holiness Christ must come from an unknown place; now we find that this one has come from Nazareth." Steeped in the literal interpretation and imitating the beliefs of fathers and ancestors they failed to understand the fact that although the body of Jesus came from Nazareth, the reality of the Christ came from the unknown place of the divine Kingdom. They also said that the sceptre of His Holiness Christ would be of iron, that is to say he should wield a sword. When His Holiness Christ appeared, he did possess a sword but it was the sword of his tongue with which he separated the false from the true; but the Jews were blind to the spiritual significance and symbolism of the prophetic words. They also expected that the Messiah would sit upon the throne of David whereas His Holiness the Christ had neither throne nor semblance of sovereignty; nay, rather, he was a poor man, apparently abject and vanquished; therefore how could he be the veritable Christ? This was one of their most insistent objections based upon ancestral interpretation and teaching. In reality His Holiness Christ was glorified with an eternal sovereignty and everlasting dominion, spiritual and not temporal. His throne and kingdom were established in human hearts where he reigns with power and authority without end. Notwithstanding the fulfillment of all the prophetic signs in His Holiness, the Jews denied him and entered the period of their deprivation because of their allegiance to imitations and ancestral forms.

Among other objections, they said, "We are promised through the tongue of the prophets that His Holiness Christ at the time of his coming would proclaim the law of the torah whereas now we see this person abrogating the commands of the pentateuch, disturbing our blessed sabbath and abolishing the law of divorce. He has left nothing of the ancient law of Moses, therefore he is the enemy of Moses." In reality His Holiness Christ proclaimed and completed the law of Moses. He was the very helper and assister of Moses. He spread the book of Moses throughout the world and established anew the fundamentals of the law revealed by him. He abolished certain unimportant laws and forms which were no longer compatible with the exigencies of the time, such as divorce and plurality of wives. The Jews did not comprehend this, and the cause of their ignorance was blind and tenacious adherence to imitations of ancient forms and teachings; therefore they finally sentenced His Holiness to death.

They likewise said, "Through the tongues of the prophets it was announced that during the time of Christ's appearance the justice of God would prevail throughout the world, tyranny and oppression would be unknown, justice would even extend to the animal kingdom, ferocious beasts would associate in gentleness and peace, the wolf and the lamb would drink from the same spring, the lion and the deer meet in the same meadow, the eagle and quail dwell together in the same nest; but instead of this, we see that during the time of this supposed Christ the Romans have conquered Palestine and are ruling it with extreme tyranny, justice is nowhere apparent and signs of peace in the kingdom are conspicuously absent." These statements and attitudes of the Jews were inherited from their fathers; blind allegiance to literal expectations which did not come to pass during the time of Jesus Christ. The real purport of these prophetic statements was that various peoples symbolized by the wolf and lamb between whom love and fellowship were impossible would come together during Messiah's reign, drink from the same fountain of life in his teachings and become his devoted followers. This was realized when peoples of all religions, nationalities and dispositions became united in their beliefs and followed Christ in humility, associating in love and brotherhood under the shadow of his divine protection. The Jews, being blind to this and holding to their bigoted imitations, were insolent and arrogant toward His Holiness and crucified him. Had they investigated the reality of Christ they would have beheld his beauty and truth.

God has given man the eye of investigation by which he may see and recognize truth. He has endowed man with ears that he may hear the message of reality and conferred upon him the gift of reason by which he may discover things for himself. This is his endowment and equipment for the investigation of reality. Man is not intended to see through the eyes of another, hear through another's ears nor comprehend with another's brain. Each human creature has individual endowment, power and responsibility in the creative plan of God. Therefore depend upon your own reason and judgment and adhere to the outcome of your own investigation; otherwise you will be utterly submerged in the sea of ignorance and deprived of all the bounties of God. Turn to God, supplicate humbly at His threshold, seeking assistance and confirmation, that God may rend asunder the veils that obscure your vision. Then will your eyes be filled with illumination, face to face you will behold the reality of God and your heart become completely purified from the dross of ignorance, reflecting the glories and bounties of the Kingdom.

Holy souls are like soil which has been plowed and tilled with much earnest labor; the thorns and thistles cast aside and all weeds uprooted. Such soil is most fruitful and the harvest from it will prove full and plenteous. In this same way man must free himself from the weeds of ignorance, thorns of superstitions and thistles of imitations, that he may discover reality in the harvests of true knowledge. Otherwise the discovery of reality is impossible, contention and divergence of religious belief will always remain and mankind, like ferocious wolves will rage and attack each other in hatred and antagonism. We supplicate God that He may destroy the veils which limit our vision and that these becloudings which darken the way of the manifestation of the shining lights may be dispelled in order that the effulgent Sun of Reality may shine forth. We implore and invoke God, seeking His assistance and confirmation. Man is a child of God; most noble, lofty and beloved by God his creator. Therefore he must ever strive that the divine bounties and virtues bestowed upon him may prevail and control him. Just now the soil of human hearts seems like black earth, but in the innermost substance of this dark soil there are thousands of fragrant flowers latent. We must endeavor to cultivate and awaken these potentialities, discover the secret treasure in this very mine and depository of God, bring forth these resplendent powers long hidden in human hearts. Then will the glories of both worlds be blended and increased and the quintessence of human existence be made manifest.

We must not be content with simply following a certain course because we find our fathers pursued that course. It is the duty of everyone to investigate reality, and investigation of reality by another will not do for us. If all in the world were rich and one man poor, of what use are these riches to that man? If all the world be virtuous and a man steeped in vice, what good results are forthcoming from him? If all the world be resplendent and a man blind, where are his benefits? If all the world be in plenty and a man hungry, what sustenance does he derive? Therefore every man must be an investigator for himself. Ideas and beliefs left by his fathers and ancestors as a heritage will not suffice, for adherence to these are but imitations and imitations have ever been a cause of disappointment and misguidance. Be investigators of reality, that you may attain the verity of truth and life.

You have asked why it was necessary for the soul that was from God to make this journey back to God. Would you like to understand the reality of this question just as I teach it or do you wish to hear it as the world teaches it?—for if I should answer you according to the latter way, this would be but imitation and would not make the subject clear.

The reality underlying this question is that the evil spirit, Satan or whatever is interpreted as evil, refers to the lower nature in man. This baser nature is symbolized in various ways. In man there are two expressions, one is the expression of nature, the other the expression of the spiritual realm. The world of nature is defective. Look at it clearly, casting aside all superstition and imagination. If you should leave a man uneducated and barbarous in the wilds of Africa, would there be any doubt about his remaining ignorant? God has never created an evil spirit; all such ideas and nomenclature are symbols expressing the mere human or earthly nature of man. It is an essential condition of the soil of earth that thorns, weeds and fruitless trees may grow from it. Relatively speaking, this is evil; it is simply the lower state and baser product of nature.

It is evident therefore that man is in need of divine education and inspiration; that the spirit and bounties of God are essential to his development. That is to say, the teachings of Christ and the prophets are necessary for his education and guidance. Why? Because they are the divine gardeners who till the earth of human hearts and minds. They educate man, uproot the weeds, burn the thorns and remodel the waste places into gardens and orchards where fruitful trees grow. The wisdom and purpose of their training is that man must pass from degree to degree of progressive unfoldment until perfection is attained. For instance, if a man should live his entire life in one city, he cannot gain a knowledge of the whole world. To become perfectly informed he must visit other cities, see the mountains and valleys, cross the rivers and traverse the plains. In other words, without progressive and universal education, perfection will not be attained.

Man must walk in many paths and be subjected to various processes in his evolution upward. Physically he is not born in full stature but passes through consecutive stages of foetus, infant, childhood, youth, maturity and old age. Suppose he had the power to remain young throughout his life. He then would not understand the meaning of old age and could not believe it existed. If he could not realize the condition of old age he would not know that he was young. He would not know the difference between young and old without experiencing the old. Unless you have passed through the state of infancy how would you know this was an infant beside you? If there was no wrong how would you recognize the right? If it were not for sin how would you appreciate virtue? If evil deeds were unknown how could you commend good actions? If sickness did not exist how would you understand health? Evil is non-existent; it is the absence of good; sickness is the loss of health; poverty the lack of riches. When wealth disappears you are poor; you look within the treasure box but find nothing there. Without knowledge there is ignorance; therefore ignorance is simply the lack of knowledge. Death is the absence of life. Therefore on the one hand we have existence; on the other, non-existence, negation or absence of existence.

Briefly; the journey of the soul is necessary. The pathway of life is the road which leads to divine knowledge and attainment. Without training and guidance the soul could never progress beyond the conditions of its lower nature which is ignorant and defective.

RELIGION:
ESSENTIAL AND NON-ESSENTIAL

THE world of existence is an emanation of the merciful attribute of God. God has shone forth upon the phenomena of being through His effulgence of mercy and He is clement and kind to all His creation. Therefore the world of humanity must ever be the recipient of bounties from the eternal Lord; even as His Holiness Christ has declared, "Be ye perfect even as your Father which is in heaven." For His bounties like the light and heat of the sun in the material heavens descend alike upon all mankind. Consequently man must learn the lesson of kindness and beneficence from God Himself. Just as God is kind to all humanity, man also must be kind to his fellow creatures. If his attitude is just and loving toward his fellow men, toward all creation, then indeed is he worthy of being pronounced the image and likeness of God.

Brotherhood or fraternity is of different kinds. It may be family association, the intimate relationship of the household. This is limited and subject to change and disruption. How often it happens that in a family, love and agreement are changed into enmity and antagonism. Another form of fraternity is manifest in patriotism. Man loves his fellow-men because they belong to the same nativity. This is also limited and subject to change and disintegration, as for instance when sons of the same fatherland are opposed to each other in war, bloodshed and battle. Still another brotherhood or fraternity is that which arises from racial unity, the oneness of racial origin, producing ties of affinity and association. This likewise has its limitation and liability to change, for often war and deadly strife have been witnessed between people and nations of the same racial lineage. There is a fourth kind of brotherhood, the attitude of man toward humanity itself, the altruistic love of humankind and recognition of the fundamental human bond. Although this is unlimited it is nevertheless susceptible to change and destruction. Even from this universal fraternal bond the looked-for result does not appear. What is the looked-for result? Loving-kindness among all human creatures and a firm, indestructible brotherhood which includes all the divine possibilities and significances in humanity. Therefore it is evident that fraternity, love and kindness based upon family, nativity, race or an attitude of altruism are neither sufficient nor permanent since all of them are limited, restricted and liable to change and disruption. For in the family there is discord and alienation; among sons of the same fatherland strife and internecine warfare are witnessed; between those of a given race, hostility and hatred are frequent; and even among the altruists varying aspects of opinion and lack of unselfish devotion give little promise of permanent and indestructible unity among mankind.

Therefore the Lord of mankind has caused His holy divine Manifestations to come into the world. He has revealed His heavenly books in order to establish spiritual brotherhood, and through the power of the Holy Spirit has made it practicable for perfect fraternity to be realized among mankind. And when through the breaths of the Holy Spirit this perfect fraternity and agreement are established amongst men, this brotherhood and love being spiritual in character, this loving-kindness being heavenly, these constraining bonds being divine, a unity appears which is indissoluble, unchanging and never subject to transformation. It is ever the same and will forever remain the same. For example consider the foundation of the brotherhood laid by His Holiness Christ. Observe how that fraternity was conducive to unity and accord and how it brought various souls to a plane of uniform attainment where they were willing to sacrifice their lives for each other. They were content to renounce possessions and ready to joyously forfeit life itself. They lived together in such love and fellowship that even Galen, the famous Greek philosopher, who was not a Christian, in his work entitled "The Progress of the Nations" says that religious beliefs are greatly conducive to the foundation of real civilization. As a proof thereof he says, "A certain number of people contemporaneous with us are known as Christians. These enjoy the superlative degree of moral civilization. Each one of them is a great philosopher because they live together in the utmost love and good-fellowship. They sacrifice life for each other. They offer worldly possessions for each other. You can say of the Christian people that they are as one person. There is a bond amongst them that is indissoluble in character."

It is evident therefore that the foundation of real brotherhood, the cause of loving co-operation and reciprocity and the source of real kindness and unselfish devotion is none other than the breaths of the Holy Spirit. Without this influence and animus it is impossible. We may be able to realize some degrees of fraternity through other motives but these are limited associations and subject to change. When human brotherhood is founded upon the Holy Spirit, it is eternal, changeless, unlimited.

In various parts of the Orient there was a time when brotherhood, loving-kindness and all the praiseworthy qualities of mankind seemed to have disappeared. There was no evidence of patriotic, religious or racial fraternity but conditions of bigotry, hatred and prejudice prevailed instead. The adherents of each religion were violent enemies of the others, filled with the spirit of hostility and eager for shedding of blood. The present war in the Balkans furnishes a parallel of these conditions. Consider the bloodshed, ferocity and oppression manifested there even in this enlightened century; all of it based fundamentally upon religious prejudice and disagreement. For the nations involved belong to the same races and nativities, nevertheless they are savage and merciless toward each other. Similar deplorable conditions prevailed in Persia in the nineteenth century. Darkness and ignorant fanaticism were widespread; no trace of fellowship or brotherhood existed amongst the races. On the contrary, human hearts were filled with rage and hatred; darkness and gloom were manifest in human lives and conditions everywhere. At such a time as this His Holiness Bahá'u'lláh appeared upon the divine horizon, even as the glory of the sun, and in that gross darkness and hopelessness of the human world there shone a great light. He founded the oneness of the world of humanity, declaring that all mankind are as sheep and that God is the real and true shepherd. The shepherd is one and all people are of his flock.

The world of humanity is one and God is equally kind to all. What then is the source of unkindness and hatred in the human world? This real shepherd loves all his sheep. He leads them in green pastures. He rears and protects them. What then is the source of enmity and alienation among humankind? Whence this conflict and strife? The real underlying cause is lack of religious unity and association for in each of the great religions we find superstition, blind imitation of creeds, and theological formulae adhered to instead of the divine fundamentals, causing difference and divergence among mankind instead of agreement and fellowship. Consequently strife, hatred and warfare have arisen, based upon this divergence and separation. If we investigate the foundations of the divine religions, we find them to be one, absolutely changeless and never subject to transformation. For example each of the divine religions contains two kinds of laws or ordinances. One division concerns the world of morality and ethical institutions. These are the essential ordinances. They instill and awaken the knowledge and love of God, love for humanity, the virtues of the world of mankind, the attributes of the divine kingdom, rebirth and resurrection from the kingdom of nature. These constitute one kind of divine law which is common to all and never subject to change. From the dawn of the Adamic cycle to the present day this fundamental law of God has continued changeless. This is the foundation of divine religion.

The second division comprises laws and institutions which provide for human needs and conditions according to exigencies of time and place. These are accidental, of no essential importance and should never have been made the cause and source of human contention. For example during the time of His Holiness Moses—Upon him be peace! —according to the exigencies of that period, divorce was permissible. During the cycle of His Holiness Christ inasmuch as divorce was not in conformity with the time and conditions His Holiness Jesus Christ abrogated it. In the cycle of Moses plurality of wives was permissible but during the time of His Holiness Christ the exigency which had sanctioned it did not exist, therefore it was forbidden. His Holiness Moses lived in the wilderness and desert of Sinai; therefore his ordinances and commandments were in conformity with those conditions. The penalty for theft was to cut off a man's hand. An ordinance of this kind was in keeping with desert life but not compatible with conditions of the present day. Such ordinances therefore constitute the second or non-essential division of the divine religions and are not of importance for they deal with human transactions which are ever changing according to the requirements of time and place. Therefore the intrinsic foundations of the divine religions are one. As this is true, why should hostility and strife exist among them? Why should this hatred and warfare, ferocity and bloodshed continue? Is this allowable and justified? God forbid!

RELIGION RENEWED

CREATION is the expression of motion. Motion is life. A moving object is a living object whereas that which is motionless and inert is as dead. All created forms are progressive in their planes or kingdoms of existence under the stimulus of the power or spirit of life. The universal energy is dynamic. Nothing is stationary in the material world of outer phenomena or in the inner world of intellect and consciousness.

Religion is the outer expression of the divine reality. Therefore it must be living, vitalized, moving and progressive. If it be without motion and non-progressive it is without the divine life; it is dead. The divine institutes are continuously active and evolutionary; therefore the revelation of them must be progressive and continuous. All things are subject to re-formation. This is a century of life and renewal. Sciences and arts, industry and invention have been reformed. Law and ethics have been reconstituted, reorganized. The world of thought has been regenerated. Sciences of former ages and philosophies of the past are useless today. Present exigencies demand new methods of solution; world problems are without precedent. Old ideas and modes of thought are fast becoming obsolete. Ancient laws and archaic ethical systems will not meet the requirements of modern conditions, for this is clearly the century of a new life, the century of the revelation of the reality and therefore the greatest of all centuries. Consider how the scientific developments of fifty years have surpassed and eclipsed the knowledge and achievements of all the former ages combined. Would the announcements and theories of ancient astronomers explain our present knowledge of the sun-worlds and planetary systems? Would the mask of obscurity which beclouded mediaeval centuries meet the demand for clear-eyed vision and understanding which characterizes the world today? In view of this, shall blind imitations of ancestral forms and theological interpretations continue to guide and control the religious life and spiritual development of humanity today? Shall man gifted with the power of reason unthinkingly follow and adhere to dogma, creeds and hereditary beliefs which will not bear the analysis of reason in this century of effulgent reality? Unquestionably this will not satisfy men of science, for when they find premise or conclusion contrary to present standards of proof and without real foundation, they reject that which has been formerly accepted as standard and correct and move forward from new foundations.

83

The divine prophets have revealed and founded religion. They have laid down certain laws and heavenly principles for the guidance of mankind. They have taught and promulgated the knowledge of God, established praiseworthy ethical ideals and inculcated the highest standards of virtue in the human world. Gradually these heavenly teachings and foundations of reality have been beclouded by human interpretations and dogmatic imitations of ancestral beliefs. The essential realities which the prophets labored so hard to establish in human hearts and minds while undergoing ordeals and suffering tortures of persecution, have now well nigh vanished. Some of these heavenly messengers have been killed, some imprisoned; all of them despised and rejected while proclaiming the reality of divinity. Soon after their departure from this world, the essential truth of their teachings was lost sight of and dogmatic imitations adhered to.

Inasmuch as human interpretations and blind imitations differ widely, religious strife and disagreement have arisen among mankind, the light of true religion has been extinguished and the unity of the world of humanity destroyed. The prophets of God voiced the spirit of unity and agreement. They have been the founders of divine reality. Therefore if the nations of the world forsake imitations and investigate the reality underlying the revealed Word of God they will agree and become reconciled. For reality is one and not multiple.

The nations and religions are steeped in blind and bigoted imitations. A man is a Jew because his father was a Jew. The Mohammedan follows implicitly the footsteps of his ancestors in belief and observance. The Buddhist is true to his heredity as a Buddhist. That is to say they profess religious belief blindly and without investigation, making unity and agreement impossible. It is evident therefore that this condition will not be remedied without a re-formation in the world of religion. In other words the fundamental reality of the divine religions must be renewed, reformed, revoiced to mankind.

From the seed of reality, religion has grown into a tree which has put forth leaves and branches, blossoms and fruit. After a time this tree has fallen into a condition of decay. The leaves and blossoms have withered and perished; the tree has become stricken and fruitless. It is not reasonable that man should hold to the old tree, claiming that its life forces are undiminished, its fruit unequalled, its existence eternal. The seed of reality must be sown again in human hearts in order that a new tree may grow therefrom and new divine fruits refresh the world. By this means the nations and peoples now divergent in religion will be brought into unity, imitations will be forsaken and a universal brotherhood in the reality itself will be established. Warfare and strife will cease among mankind; all will be reconciled as servants of God. For all are sheltered beneath the tree of His providence and mercy. God is kind to all; He is the giver of bounty to all alike, even as His Holiness Jesus Christ has declared that God "sendeth rain on the just and on the unjust;" that is to say, the mercy of God is universal. All humanity is under the protection of His love and favor, and unto all He has pointed the way of guidance and progress.

Progress is of two kinds, material and spiritual. The former is attained through observation of the surrounding existence and constitutes the foundation of civilization. Spiritual progress is through the breaths of the Holy Spirit and is the awakening of the conscious soul of man to perceive the reality of divinity. Material progress insures the happiness of the human world. Spiritual progress insures the happiness and eternal continuance of the soul. The prophets of God have founded the laws of divine civilization. They have been the root and fundamental source of all knowledge. They have established the principles of human brotherhood or fraternity which is of various kinds, such as the fraternity of family, of race, of nation and of ethical motives. These forms of fraternity, these bonds of brotherhood are merely temporal and transient in association. They do not insure harmony and are usually productive of disagreement. They do not prevent warfare and strife; on the contrary they are selfish, restricted and fruitful causes of enmity and hatred among mankind. The spiritual brotherhood which is enkindled and established through the breaths of the Holy Spirit unites nations and removes the cause of warfare and strife. It transforms mankind into one great family and establishes the foundations of the oneness of humanity. It promulgates the spirit of international agreement and insures universal peace. Therefore we must investigate the foundation reality of this heavenly fraternity. We must forsake all imitations and promote the reality of the divine teachings. In accordance with these principles and actions and by the assistance of the Holy Spirit, both material and spiritual happiness shall become realized. Until all nations and peoples become united by the bonds of the Holy Spirit in this real fraternity, until national and international prejudices are effaced in the reality of this spiritual brotherhood, true progress, prosperity and lasting happiness will not be attained by man. This is the century of new and universal nationhood. Sciences have advanced, industries have progressed, politics have been reformed, liberty has been proclaimed, justice is awakening. This is the century of motion, divine stimulus and accomplishment; the century of human solidarity and altruistic service; the century of universal peace and the reality of the divine Kingdom.

DIVINE LOVE

EVERY subject presented to a thoughtful audience must be supported by rational proofs and logical arguments. Proofs are of four kinds: first, through sense-perception; second, through the reasoning faculty; third, from traditional or scriptural authority; fourth, through the medium of inspiration. That is to say, there are four criterions or standards of judgment by which the human mind reaches its conclusions. We will first consider the criterion of the senses. This is a standard still held to by the materialistic philosophers of the world. They believe that whatever is perceptible to the senses is a verity, a certainty and without doubt existent. For example, they say, "Here is a lamp which you see, and because it is perceptible to the sense of sight you cannot doubt its existence. There is a tree; your sense of vision assures you of its reality which is beyond question. This is a man; you see that he is a man; therefore he exists." In a word, everything confirmed by the senses is assumed to be as undoubted and unquestioned as the product of five multiplied by five; it cannot be twenty-six nor less than twenty-five. Consequently the materialistic philosophers consider the criterion of the senses to be first and foremost.

But in the estimation of the divine philosophers this proof and assurance is not reliable; nay, rather, they deem the standard of the senses to be false because it is imperfect. Sight, for instance, is one of the most important of the senses, yet it is subject to many aberrations and inaccuracies. The eye sees the mirage as a body of water, regards images in the mirror as realities when they are but reflections. A man sailing upon the river imagines that objects upon the shore are moving whereas he is in motion and they are stationary. To the eye the earth appears fixed while the sun and stars revolve about it. As a matter of fact the heavenly orbs are stationary and the earth turning upon its axis. The colossal suns, planets and constellations which shine in the heavens appear small, nay, infinitesimal to human vision whereas in reality they are vastly greater than the earth in dimension and volume. A whirling spark appears to the sight as a circle of fire. There are numberless instances of this kind which show the error and inaccuracy of the senses. Therefore the divine philosophers have considered this standard of judgment to be defective and unreliable.

The second criterion is that of the intellect. The ancient philosophers in particular considered the intellect to be the most important agency of judgment. Among the wise men of Greece, Rome, Persia and Egypt the criterion of true proof was reason. They held that every matter submitted to the reasoning faculty could be proved true or false and must be accepted or rejected accordingly. But in the estimation of the people of insight this criterion is likewise defective and unreliable, for these same philosophers who held to reason or intellect as the standard of human judgment have differed widely among themselves upon every subject of investigation. The statements of the Greek philosophers are contradictory to the conclusions of the Persian sages. Even among the Greek philosophers themselves there is continual variance and lack of agreement upon any given subject. Great difference of thought also prevailed between the wise men of Greece and Rome. Therefore if the criterion of reason or intellect constituted a correct and infallible standard of judgment, those who tested and applied it should have arrived at the same conclusions. As they differ and are contradictory in conclusions it is an evidence that the method and standard of test must have been faulty and insufficient.

The third criterion or standard of proof is traditional or scriptural, namely, that every statement of conclusion should be supported by traditions recorded in certain religious books. When we come to consider even the holy books—the books of God—we are led to ask, "Who understands these books? By what authority of explanation may these books be understood?" It must be the authority of human reason, and if reason or intellect finds itself incapable of explaining certain questions, or if the possessors of intellect contradict each other in the interpretation of traditions, how can such a criterion be relied upon for accurate conclusions?

The fourth standard is that of inspiration. In past centuries many philosophers have claimed illumination or revelation, prefacing their statements by the announcement that "this subject has been revealed through me" or "thus do I speak by inspiration." Of this class were the philosophers of the Illuminati. Inspirations are the promptings or susceptibilities of the human heart. The promptings of the heart are sometimes satanic. How are we to differentiate them? How are we to tell whether a given statement is an inspiration and prompting of the heart through the merciful assistance or through the satanic agency?

Consequently it has become evident that the four criterions or standards of judgment by which the human mind reaches its conclusions are faulty and inaccurate. All of them are liable to mistake and error in conclusions. But a statement presented to the mind accompanied by proofs which the senses can perceive to be correct, which the faculty of reason can accept, which is in accord with traditional authority and sanctioned by the promptings of the heart, can be adjudged and relied upon as perfectly correct, for it has been proved and tested by all the standards of judgment and found to be complete. When we apply but one test there are possibilities of mistake. This is self-evident and manifest.

We will now consider the subject of "Love" which has been suggested, submitting it to the four standards of judgment and thereby reaching our conclusions.

We declare that love is the cause of the existence of all phenomena and that the absence of love is the cause of disintegration or non-existence. Love is the conscious bestowal of God, the bond of affiliation in all phenomena. We will first consider the proof of this through sense-perception. As we look upon the universe we observe that all composite beings or existing phenomena are made up primarily of single elements bound together by a power of attraction. Through this power of attraction, cohesion has become manifest between atoms of these composing elements. The resultant being is a phenomenon of the lower contingent type. The power of cohesion expressed in the mineral kingdom is in reality love or affinity manifested in a low degree according to the exigencies of the mineral world. We take a step higher into the vegetable kingdom where we find an increased power of attraction has become manifest among the composing elements which form phenomena. Through this degree of attraction a cellular admixture is produced among these elements which make up the body of a plant. Therefore in the degree of the vegetable kingdom there is love. We enter the animal kingdom and find the attractive power binding together single elements as in the mineral, plus the cellular admixture as in the vegetable, plus the phenomena of feelings or susceptibilities. We observe that the animals are susceptible to certain affiliation and fellowship, and that they exercise natural selection. This elemental attraction, this admixture and selective affinity is love manifest in the degree of the animal kingdom.

Finally we come to the kingdom of man. As this is the superior kingdom, the light of love is more resplendent. In man we find the power of attraction among the elements which compose his material body, plus the attraction which produces cellular admixture or power augmentative, plus the attraction which characterizes the sensibilities of the animal kingdom, but still beyond and above all these lower powers we discover in the being of man the attraction of heart, the susceptibilities and affinities which bind men together, enabling them to live and associate in friendship and solidarity. It is therefore evident that in the world of humanity the greatest king and sovereign is love. If love were extinguished, the power of attraction dispelled, the affinity of human hearts destroyed, the phenomena of human life would disappear.

This is a proof perceptible to the senses, acceptable to reason, in accord with traditions and teachings of the holy books and verified by the promptings of human hearts themselves. It is a proof upon which we can absolutely rely and declare to be complete. But these are only degrees of love which exist in the natural or physical world. Their manifestation is ever according to the requirement of natural conditions and standards.

Real love is the love which exists between God and His servants, the love which binds together holy souls. This is the love of the spiritual world, not the love of physical bodies and organisms. For example, consider and observe how the bestowals of God successively descend upon mankind; how the divine effulgences ever shine upon the human world. There can be no doubt that these bestowals, these bounties, these effulgences emanate from love. Unless love be the divine motive, it would be impossible for the heart of man to attain or receive them. Unless love exists the divine blessing could not descend upon any object or thing. Unless there be love the recipient of divine effulgence could not radiate and reflect that effulgence upon other objects. If we are of those who perceive, we realize that the bounties of God manifest themselves continuously, even as the rays of the sun unceasingly emanate from the solar center. The phenomenal world through the resplendent effulgence of the sun is radiant and bright. In the same way the realm of hearts and spirits is illumined and re-suscitated through the shining rays of the Sun of Reality and the bounties of the love of God. Thereby the world of existence, the king-dom of hearts and spirits is ever quickened into life. Were it not for the love of God, hearts would be inanimate, spirits would wither and the reality of man would be bereft of the everlasting bestowals.

Consider to what extent the love of God makes itself manifest. Among the signs of His love which appear in the world are the dawn-ing-point of His Manifestations. What an infinite degree of love is reflected by the divine Manifestations toward mankind! For the sake of guiding the people they have willingly forfeited their lives to resuscitate human hearts. They have accepted the cross. To enable human souls to attain the supreme degree of advancement, they have suffered during their limited years extreme ordeals and difficulties. If His Holiness Jesus Christ had not possessed love for the world of humanity, surely he would not have welcomed the cross. He was crucified for the love of mankind. Consider the infinite degree of that love. Without love for humanity John the Baptist would not have offered his life. It has been likewise with all the prophets and holy souls. If His Holiness the Bab had not manifested love for mankind, surely he would not have offered his breast for a thousand bullets. If His Holiness Bahá'u'lláh had not been aflame with love for humanity he would not have willingly accepted forty years' imprisonment.

Observe how rarely human souls sacrifice their pleasure or comfort for others; how improbable that a man would offer his eye or suffer himself to be dismembered for the benefit of another. Yet all the divine Manifestations suffered, offered their lives and blood, sacrificed their existence, comfort and all they possessed for the sake of mankind. Therefore consider how much they love. Were it not for their love for humanity, spiritual love would be mere nomenclature. Were it not for their illumination, human souls would not be radiant. How effective is their love! This is a sign of the love of God; a ray of the Sun of Reality.

Therefore we must give praise unto God, for it is the light of His bounty which has shone upon us through His love which is everlasting. His divine Manifestations have offered their lives through love for us. Consider then what the love of God means. Were it not for the love of God all the spirits would be inanimate. The meaning of this is not physical death; nay, rather, it is that condition concerning which His Holiness Christ declared, "Let the dead bury their dead, for that which is born of the flesh is flesh, and that which is born of the spirit is spirit." Were it not for the love of God the hearts would not be illumined. Were it not for the love of God the pathway of the Kingdom would not be opened. Were it not for the love of God the holy books would not have been revealed. Were it not for the love of God the divine prophets would not have been sent to the world. The foundation of all these bestowals is the love of God. Therefore in the human world there is no greater power than the love of God. It is the love of God which has brought us together here tonight. It is the love of God which is affiliating the East and the West. It is the love of God which has resuscitated the world. Now we must offer thanks to God that such a great bestowal and effulgence has been revealed to us.

We come to another aspect of our subject—Are the workings and effects of love confined to this world or do they extend on and on to another existence? Will its influence affect our existence here only or will it extend to the life everlasting? When we look upon the human kingdom we readily observe that it is superior to all others. In the differentiation of life in the world of existence, there are four degrees or kingdoms,—the mineral, vegetable, animal, and human. The mineral kingdom is possessed of a certain virtue which we term cohesion. The vegetable kingdom possesses cohesive properties plus the power of growth or power augmentative. The animal kingdom is possessed of the virtues of the mineral and vegetable plus the powers of the senses. But the animal although gifted with sensibilities is utterly bereft of consciousness, absolutely out of touch with the world of consciousness and spirit. The animal possesses no powers by which it can make discoveries which lie beyond the realm of the senses. It has no power of intellectual origination. For example, an animal located in Europe is not capable of discovering the continent of America. It understands only phenomena which come within the range of its senses and instinct. It cannot abstractly reason out anything. The animal cannot conceive of the earth being spherical or revolving upon its axis. It cannot apprehend that the little stars in the heavens are tremendous worlds vastly greater than the earth. The animal cannot abstractly conceive of intellect. Of these powers it is bereft. Therefore these powers are peculiar to man and it is made evident that in the human kingdom there is a reality of which the animal is minus. What is that reality? It is the spirit of man. By it man is distinguished above all the other phenomenal kingdoms. Although he possesses all the virtues of the lower kingdoms he is further endowed with the spiritual faculty, the heavenly gift of consciousness.

All material phenomena are subject to nature. All material organisms are captives of nature. None of them can deviate in the slightest from the law of nature. This earth, these great mountains, the animals with their wonderful powers and instincts cannot go beyond natural limitations. All things are captives of nature except man. Man is the sovereign of nature; he breaks nature's laws. Though an animal fitted by nature to live upon the surface of the earth he flies in the air like a bird, sails upon the ocean and dives deep beneath its waves in submarines. Man is gifted with a power whereby he penetrates and discovers the laws of nature, brings them forth from the world of invisibility into the plane of visibility. Electricity was once a latent force of nature. According to nature's laws it should remain a hidden secret, but the spirit of man discovered it, brought it forth from its secret depository and made its phenomena visible. It is evident and manifest that man is capable of breaking nature's laws. How does he accomplish it? Through a spirit with which God has endowed him at creation. This is a proof that the spirit of man differentiates and distinguishes him above all the lower kingdoms. It is this spirit to which the verse in the Old Testament refers when it states that man has been created "after the image and likeness of God". The spirit of man alone penetrates the realities of God and partakes of the divine bounties.

THE FOUNDATION OF RELIGION

GOD is one; the effulgence of God is one; and humanity constitutes the servants of that one God. God is kind to all. He creates and provides for all; and all are under His care and protection. The Sun of Truth, the Word of God shines upon all mankind; the divine cloud pours down its precious rain; the gentle zephyrs of His mercy blow and all humanity is submerged in the ocean of His eternal justice and loving-kindness.

But we have acted contrary to the will and good-pleasure of God. We have been the cause of enmity and disunion. We have separated from each other and risen against each other in opposition and strife. How many have been the wars between peoples and nations! What bloodshed! Numberless are the cities and homes which have been laid waste. All of this has been contrary to the good-pleasure of God for He hath willed love for humanity. He is clement and merciful to all His creatures. He hath ordained amity and fellowship amongst men.

Most regrettable of all is the state of difference and divergence we have created between each other in the name of religion imagining that a paramount duty in our religious belief is that of alienation and estrangement, that we should shun each other and consider each other contaminated with error and infidelity. In reality the foundations of the divine religions are one and the same. The differences which have arisen between us are due to blind imitations of dogmatic beliefs and adherence to ancestral forms of worship. His Holiness Abraham was the founder of reality. His Holiness Moses, His Holiness Christ, His Holiness Mohammed were the manifestations of reality. His Holiness Bahá'u'lláh was the glory of reality. This is not simply an assertion; it will be proved.

Let me ask your closest attention in considering this subject. The divine religions embody two kinds of ordinances. First, those which constitute essential or spiritual teachings of the Word of God. These are faith in God, the acquirement of the virtues which characterize perfect manhood, praiseworthy moralities, the acquisition of the bestowals and bounties emanating from the divine effulgences; in brief, the ordinances which concern the realm of morals and ethics. This is the fundamental aspect of the religion of God and this is of the highest importance because knowledge of God is the fundamental requirement of man. Man must comprehend the oneness of divinity. He must come to know and acknowledge the precepts of God and realize for a certainty that the ethical development of humanity is dependent upon religion. He must get rid of all defects and seek the attainment of heavenly virtues in order that he may prove to be the image and likeness of God. It is recorded in the holy bible that God said, "Let us make man in our image, after our likeness." It is self-evident that the image and likeness mentioned do not apply to the form and semblance of a human being because the reality of divinity is not limited to any form or figure. Nay, rather the attributes and characteristics of God are intended. Even as God is pronounced to be just, man must likewise be just. As God is loving and kind to all men, man must likewise manifest loving-kindness to all humanity. As God is loyal and truthful, man must show forth the same attributes in the human world. Even as God exercises mercy toward all, man must prove himself to be the manifestation of mercy. In a word, the "image and likeness of God" constitute the virtues of God, and man is intended to become the recipient of the effulgences of divine attributes. This is the essential foundation of all the divine religions, the reality itself, common to all. His Holiness Abraham promulgated this; His Holiness Moses proclaimed it. His Holiness Christ and all the prophets upheld this standard and aspect of divine religion.

Secondly: Laws and ordinances which are temporary and non-essential. These concern human transactions and relations. They are accidental and subject to change according to the exigencies of time and place. These ordinances are neither permanent nor fundamental. For instance during the time of Noah it was expedient that sea foods be considered as lawful; therefore God commanded Noah to partake of all marine animal life. During the time of Moses this was not in accordance with the exigencies of Israel's existence, therefore a second command was revealed partly abrogating the law concerning marine foods. During the time of Abraham—Upon him be peace!—camel's milk was considered a lawful and acceptable food; likewise the flesh of the camel; but during Jacob's time because of a certain vow he made, this became unlawful. These are non-essential temporary laws. In the holy bible there are certain commandments which according to those bygone times constituted the very spirit of the age, the very light of that period. For example according to the law of the torah if a man committed theft of a certain amount they cut off his hand. Is it practicable and reasonable in this present day to cut off a man's hand for the theft of a dollar? In the torah there are ten ordinances concerning murder. Could these be made effective today? Unquestionably no; times have changed. According to the explicit text of the bible if a man should change or break the law of the Sabbath or if he should touch fire on the Sabbath he must be killed. Today such a law is abrogated. The torah declares that if a man should speak a disrespectful word to his father he should suffer the penalty of death. Is this possible of enforcement now? No; human conditions have undergone changes. Likewise during the time of Christ certain minor ordinances conformable to that period were enforced.

It has been shown conclusively therefore that the foundation of the religion of God remains permanent and unchanging. It is that fixed foundation which insures the progress and stability of the body politic and the illumination of humanity. It has ever been the cause of love and justice amongst men. It works for the true fellowship and unification of all mankind for it never changes and is not subject to supersedure. The accidental or non-essential laws which regulate the transactions of the social body and everyday affairs of life are changeable and subject to abrogation.

Let me ask what is the purpose of prophethood? Why has God sent the prophets? It is self-evident that the prophets are the educators of men and the teachers of the human race. They come to bestow universal education upon humanity, to give humanity training, to uplift the human race from the abyss of despair and desolation and enable man to attain the apogee of advancement and glory. The people are in darkness; the prophets bring them into the realm of light. They are in a state of utter imperfection; the prophets imbue them with perfections. The purpose of the prophetic mission is no other than the education and guidance of the people. Therefore we must regard and be on the lookout for the man who is thus qualified; that is to say any soul who proves to be the educator of mankind and the teacher of the human race is undoubtedly the prophet of his age.

For example let us review the events connected with the history of His Holiness Moses—Upon him be peace! His Holiness dwelt in Midian at a time when the children of Isarel were in captivity and bondage in the land of Egypt, subjected to every tyranny and severe oppression. They were illiterate and ignorant, undergoing cruel ordeals and experiences. They were in such a state of helplessness and impotence that it was proverbial to state that one Egyptian could overcome ten Israelites. At such a time as this and under such forbidding conditions His Holiness Moses appeared and shone forth with a heavenly radiance. He saved Israel from the bondage of Pharaoh and released them from captivity. He led them out of the land of Egypt and into the Holy Land. They had been scattered and broken; he unified and disciplined them; conferred upon them the blessing of wisdom and knowledge. They had been slaves; he made them princes. They were ignorant; he made them learned; they were imperfect; he enabled them to attain perfection. In a word—he led them out of their condition of hopelessness and brought them to efficiency in the plane of confidence and valor. They became renowned throughout the ancient world until finally in the zenith and splendor of their new civilization the glory of the sovereignty of Solomon was attained. Through the guidance and training of His Holiness Moses these slaves and captives became the dominating people amongst the nations. Not only in physical and military superiority were they renowned but in all the degrees of arts, letters and refinement their fame was widespread. Even the celebrated philosophers of Greece journeyed to Jerusalem in order to study with the Israelitish sages and many were the lessons of philosophy and wisdom they received. Among these philosophers was the famous Socrates. He visited the Holy Land and studied with the prophets of Israel, acquiring principles of their philosophical teaching and a knowledge of their advanced arts and sciences. After his return to Greece he founded the system known as the unity of God. The Greek people rose against him and at last he was poisoned in the presence of the king. Hippocrates and many other Greek philosophers sat at the feet of the learned Israelitish doctors and absorbed their expositions of wisdom and the inner truth.

Inasmuch as His Holiness Moses through the influence of his great mission was instrumental in releasing the Israelites from a low state of debasement and humiliation, establishing them in a station of prestige and glorification, disciplining and educating them, it is necessary for us to reach a fair and just judgment in regard to such a marvelous teacher. For in this great accomplishment he stood single and alone. Could he have made such a change and brought about such a condition among these people without the sanction and assistance of a heavenly power? Could he have transformed a people from humiliation to glory without a holy and divine support?

No other than a divine power could have done this. Therein lies the proof of prophethood because the mission of a prophet is education of the human race such as this personage accomplished, proving him to be a mighty prophet among the prophets, and his book the very Book of God. This is a rational, direct and perfect proof.

In brief, His Holiness Moses—Upon whom be peace!—founded the law of God, purified the morals of the people of Israel and gave them an impetus toward nobler and higher attainments. But after the departure of His Holiness Moses, following the decline of the glory of Solomon's era and during the reign of Jeroboam there came a great change in this nation. The high ethical standards and spiritual perfections ceased to exist. Conditions and morals became corrupt, religion was debased and the perfect principles of the Mosaic law were obscured in superstition and polytheism. War and strife arose among the tribes and their unity was destroyed. The followers of Jeroboam declared themselves rightful and valid in kingly succession, and the supporters of Rehoboam made the same claim. Finally the tribes were torn asunder by hostility and hatred, the glory of Israel was eclipsed and so complete was the degradation, that a golden calf was set up as an object of worship in the city of Tyre. Thereupon God sent Elijah the prophet who redeemed the people, renewed the law of God and established an era of new life for Israel. History shows a still later change and transformation when this oneness and solidarity were followed by another dispersion of the tribes. Nebuchadnezzar, king of Babylon, invaded the Holy Land and carried away captive seventy thousand Israelites to Chaldea where the greatest reverses, trials and suffering afflicted these unfortunate people. Then the prophets of God again reformed and re-established the law of God and the people in their humiliation again followed it. This resulted in their liberation, and under the edict of Cyrus, king of Persia, there was a return to the holy city. Jerusalem and the temple of Solomon were rebuilt and the glory of Israel was restored. This lasted but a short time; the morality of the people declined and conditions reached an extreme degree until the Roman general Titus took Jerusalem and razed it to its foundations. Pillage and conquest completed the desolation; Palestine became a waste and wilderness and the Jews fled from the Holy Land of their ancestors. The cause of this disintegration and dispersion was the departure of Israel from the foundation of the law of God revealed by Moses, namely the acquisition of divine virtues, morality, love, the development of arts and sciences and the spirit of the oneness of humanity.

I now wish you* to examine certain facts and statements which are worthy of consideration. My purpose and intention is to remove from the hearts of men the religious enmity and hatred which have fettered them and to bring all religions into agreement and unity. Inasmuch as this hatred and enmity, this bigotry and intolerance are outcomes of misunderstandings, the reality of religious unity will appear when these misunderstandings are dispelled. For the foundation of the divine religions is one foundation. This is the oneness of revelation or teaching; but alas! we have turned away from that foundation, holding tenaciously to various dogmatic forms and blind imitation of ancestral beliefs. This is the real cause of enmity, hatred and bloodshed in the world; the reason of alienation and estrangement among mankind. Therefore I wish you to be very just and fair in your judgment of the following statements.

During the time that the people of Israel were being tossed and

---

*The congregation of Eighth Street Temple, Washington, D.C.

afflicted by the conditions I have named, His Holiness Jesus Christ appeared among them. Jesus of Nazareth was a Jew. He was single and unaided, alone and unique. He had no assistant. The Jews at once pronounced him to be an enemy of Moses. They declared that he was the destroyer of the Mosaic laws and ordinances. Let us examine the facts as they are, investigate the truth and reality in order to arrive at a true opinion and conclusion. For a completely fair opinion upon this question we must lay aside all we have and investigate independently. This personage Jesus Christ declared His Holiness Moses to have been the prophet of God and pronounced all the prophets of Israel as sent from God. He proclaimed the torah the very Book of God, summoned all to conform to its precepts and follow its teachings. It is a historical fact that during a period of fifteen hundred years the kings of Israel were unable to promulgate broadcast the religion of Judaism. In fact during that period the name and history of Moses were confined to the boundaries of Palestine and the torah was a book well known only in that country. But through His Holiness Christ, through the blessing of the New Testament of Jesus Christ, the Old Testament, the torah, was translated into six hundred different tongues and spread throughout the world. It was through Christianity that the torah reached Persia. Before that time there was no knowledge in that country of such a book, but His Holiness Christ caused its spread and acceptance. Through him the name of Moses was elevated and revered. He was instrumental in publishing the name and greatness of the Isarelitish prophets and he proved to the world that the Israelites constituted the people of God. Which of the kings of Israel could have accomplished this? Were it not for Jesus Christ would the bible, the torah, have reached this land of America? Would the name of Moses be spread throughout the world? Refer to history. Everyone knows that when Christianity was spread, there was a simultaneous spread of the knowledge of Judaism and the torah. Throughout the length and breadth of Persia there was not a single volume of the Old Testament until the religion of Jesus Christ caused it to appear everywhere, so that today the holy bible is a household book in that country. It is evident then that Christ was a friend of Moses, that he loved and believed in His Holiness Moses, otherwise he would not have commemorated his name and prophethood. This is self-evident. Therefore Christians and Jews should have the greatest love for each other because the founders of these two great religions have been in perfect agreement in book and teaching. Their followers should be likewise.

We have already stated the valid proofs of prophethood. We find the very evidences of the validity of His Holiness Moses were witnessed and duplicated in His Holiness Christ. His Holiness Christ was also a unique and single personage born of the lineage of Israel. By the power of his Word he was able to unite people of the Roman, Greek, Chaldean, Egyptian and Assyrian nations. Whereas they had been cruel, bloodthirsty and hostile, killing, pillaging and taking each other captive, he cemented them together in a perfect bond of unity and love. He caused them to agree and become reconciled. Such mighty effects were the results of the manifestation of one single soul. This proves conclusively that His Holiness Christ was assisted by God. Today all Christians admit and believe that His Holiness Moses was a prophet of God. They declare that his book was the Book of God, that the prophets of Israel were true and valid and that the people of Israel constituted the people of God. What harm has come from this? What harm could come from a statement by the Jews that Jesus was also a manifestation of the Word of God? Have the Christians suffered for their belief in Moses? Have they experienced any loss of religious enthusiasm or witnessed any defeat in their religious belief by declaring that His Holiness Moses was a prophet of God, that the torah was a Book of God and that all the prophets of Israel were prophets of God? It is evident that no loss comes from this. And now it is time for the Jews to declare that Christ was the Word of God and then this enmity between two great religions will pass away. For two thousand years this enmity and religious prejudice have continued. Blood has been shed, ordeals have been suffered. These few words will remedy the difficulty and unite two great religions. What harm could follow this,—that just as the Christians glorify and praise the name of Moses, likewise the Jews should commemorate the name of Christ, declare him to be the Word of God and consider him as one of the chosen messengers of God?

A few words concerning the koran and the Mohammedans: When His Holiness Mohammed appeared he spoke of Moses as the great man of God. In the koran he refers to the sayings of Moses in seven different places, proclaims him a prophet and the possessor of a Book, the founder of the law, and the spirit of God. He said, "Whosoever believes in him is acceptable in the estimation of God and whosoever shuns him or any of the prophets is rejected of God." Even in conclusion he calls upon his own relatives, saying, "Why have ye shunned and not believed in Moses? Why have ye not acknowledged the torah? Why have ye not believed in the Jewish prophets?" In a certain surat of the koran he mentions the names of twenty-eight of the prophets of Israel, praising each and all of them. To this great extent he has ratified and commended the prophets and religion of Israel. The purport is this,—that Mohammed praised and glorified His Holiness Moses and confirmed Judaism. He declared that whosoever denies Moses is contaminated and even if he repents, his repentance will not be accepted. He pronounced his own relatives infidels and impure because they had denied the prophets. He said, "Because you have not believed in Christ, because you have not believed in Moses, because you have not believed in the gospels you are infidels and contaminated." In this way Mohammed has praised the torah, Moses, Christ and the prophets of the past. He appeared amongst the Arabs who were a people nomadic and illiterate, barbarous in nature and blood-thirsty. He guided and trained them until they attained a high degree of development. Through his education and discipline they rose from the lowest levels of ignorance to the heights of knowledge, becoming masters of erudition and philosophy. We see therefore that the proofs applicable to one prophet are equally applicable to another.

In conclusion; since the prophets themselves, the founders, have loved, praised and testified of each other, why should we disagree and be alienated? God is one. He is the shepherd of all. We are his sheep and therefore should live together in love and unity. We should manifest the spirit of justness and good-will toward each other. Shall we do this or shall we censure and pronounce anathema, praising ourselves and condemning all others? What possible good can come from such attitude and action? On the contrary, nothing but enmity and hatred, injustice and inhumanity can possibly result. Has not this been the greatest cause of bloodshed, woe and tribulation in the past?

Praise be to God! You are living in a land of freedom. You are blessed with men of learning, men who are well versed in the comparative study of religions. You realize the need of unity and know the great harm which comes from prejudice and superstition. I ask you, Is not fellowship and brotherhood preferable to enmity and hatred in society and community? The answer is self-evident. Love and fellowship are absolutely needful to win the good-pleasure of God which is the goal of all human attainment. We must be united. We must love each other. We must ever praise each other. We must bestow commendation upon all people, thus removing the discord and hatred which have caused alienation amongst men. Otherwise the conditions of the past will continue, praising ourselves and condemning others; religious wars will have no end and religious prejudice, the prime cause of this havoc and tribulation, will increase. This must be abandoned, and the way to do it is to investigate the reality which underlies all the religions. This underlying reality is the love of humanity. For God is one and humanity is one, and the only creed of the prophets is love and unity.

THE QUICKENING SPIRIT

TODAY the human world is in need of a great power by which these glorious principles and purposes may be executed. The cause of peace is a very great cause; it is the cause of God, and all the forces of the world are opposed to it. Governments for instance, consider militarism as the step to human progress, that division among men and nations is the cause of patriotism and honor, that if one nation attack and conquer another, gaining wealth, territory and glory thereby, this warfare and conquest, this bloodshed and cruelty are the cause of that victorious nation's advancement and prosperity. This is an utter mistake. Compare the nations of the world to the members of a family. A family is a nation in miniature. Simply enlarge the circle of the household and you have the nation. Enlarge the circle of nations and you have all humanity. The conditions surrounding the family surround the nation. The happenings in the family are the happenings in the life of the nation. Would it add to the progress and advancement of a family if dissensions should arise among its members, fighting, pillaging each other, jealous and revengeful of injury, seeking selfish advantage? Nay, this would be the cause of the effacement of progress and advancement. So it is in the great family of nations, for nations are but an aggregate of families. Therefore as strife and dissension destroy a family and prevent its progress, so nations are destroyed and advancement hindered.

All the heavenly books, divine prophets, sages and philosophers agree that warfare is destructive to human development, and peace constructive. They agree that war and strife strike at the foundations of humanity. Therefore a power is needed to prevent war and to proclaim and establish the oneness of humanity.

But knowledge of the need of this power is not sufficient. Realizing that wealth is desirable is not becoming wealthy. The admission that scientific attainment is praiseworthy does not confer scientific knowledge. Acknowledgment of the excellence of honor does not make a man honorable. Knowledge of human conditions and the needed remedy for them is not the cause of their betterment. To admit that health is good does not constitute health. A skilled physician is needed to remedy existing human conditions. As a physician is required to have complete knowledge of pathology, diagnosis, therapeutics and treatment, so this world physician must be wise, skillful and capable before health will result. His mere knowledge is not health; it must be applied and the remedy carried out.

The attainment of any object is conditioned upon knowledge, volition and action. Unless these three conditions are forthcoming there is no execution or accomplishment. In the erection of a house it is first necessary to know the ground and design the house suitable for it; second, to obtain the means or funds necessary for the construction; third, to actually build it. Therefore a power is needed to carry out and execute what is known and admitted to be the remedy for human conditions; namely, the unification of mankind. Furthermore, it is evident that this cannot be realized through material process and means. The accomplishment of this unification cannot be through racial power, for races are different and diverse in tendencies. It cannot be through patriotic power, for nationalities are unlike. Nor can it be effected through political power since the policies of governments and nations are various. That is to say, any effort toward unification through these material means would benefit one and injure another because of unequal and individual interests. Some may believe this great remedy can be found in dogmatic insistence upon imitations and interpretations. This would likewise be without foundation and result. Therefore it is evident that no means but an ideal means, a spiritual power, divine bestowals and the breaths of the Holy Spirit will heal this world sickness of war, dissension and discord. Nothing else is possible; nothing can be conceived of. But through spiritual means and the divine power it is possible and practicable.

Consider history. What has brought unity to nations, morality to peoples and benefits to mankind? If we reflect upon it we will find that establishing the divine religions has been the greatest means toward accomplishing the oneness of humanity. The foundation of divine reality in religion has done this; not imitations of ancestral religious forms. Imitations are opposed to each other and have ever been the cause of strife, enmity, jealousy and war. The divine religions are collective centers in which diverse standpoints may meet, agree and unify. They accomplish oneness of nativities, races and policies. For instance, His Holiness Christ united various nations, brought peace to warring peoples and established the oneness of human kind. The conquering Greeks and Romans, the prejudiced Egyptians and Assyrians were all in a condition of strife, enmity and war but His Holiness gathered these varied peoples together and removed the foundations of discord; not through racial, patriotic or political power but through divine power, the power of the Holy Spirit. This was not otherwise possible. All other efforts of men and nations remain as mere mention in history, without accomplishment.

As this great result is contingent upon divine power and bestowals, where shall the world obtain that power? God is eternal and ancient; not a new God. His sovereignty is of old, not recent; not merely existent these five or six thousand years. This infinite universe is from everlasting. The sovereignty, power, names and attributes of God are eternal, ancient. His names presuppose creation and predicate His existence and will. We say God is creator. This name creator appears when we connote creation. We say God is the provider. This name presupposes and proves the existence of the provided. God is love. This name proves the existence of the beloved. In the same way God is mercy, God is justice, God is life, etc., etc. Therefore as God is creator, eternal and ancient, there were always creatures and subjects existing and provided for. There is no doubt that divine sovereignty is eternal. Sovereignty necessitates subjects, ministers, trustees and others subordinate to sovereignty. Could there be a king without country, subjects and armies? If we conceive of a time when there were no creatures, no servants, no subjects of divine lordship we dethrone God and predicate a time when God was not. It would be as if He had been recently appointed and man had given these names to Him. The divine sovereignty is ancient, eternal. God from everlasting was love, justice, power, creator, provider, the omniscient, the bountiful.

As the divine entity is eternal, the divine attributes are coexistent, co-eternal. The divine bestowals are therefore without beginning, without end. God is infinite; the works of God are infinite; the bestowals of God are infinite. As His divinity is eternal, His lordship and perfections are without end. As the bounty of the Holy Spirit is eternal, we can never say that His bestowals terminate, else He terminates. If we think of the sun and then try to conceive of the cessation of the solar flame and heat, we have predicated the non-existence of the sun. For separation of the sun from its rays and heat is inconceivable. Therefore if we limit the bestowals of God we limit the attributes of God and limit God.

Let us then trust in the bounty and bestowal of God. Let us be exhilarated with the divine breath, illumined and exalted by the heavenly glad-tidings. God has ever dealt with man in mercy and kindness. He who conferred the divine spirit in former times is abundantly able and capable at all times and periods to grant the same bestowals. Therefore let us be hopeful. The God who gave to the world formerly will do so now and in the future. God who breathed the breath of the Holy Spirit upon His servants will breathe it upon them now and hereafter. There is no cessation to His bounty. The divine spirit is penetrating from eternity to eternity for it is the bounty of God and the bounty of God is eternal. Can you conceive of limitation of the divine power in atomic verities or cessation of the divine bounty in existing organisms? Could you conceive the power now manifest in this glass in cohesion of its atoms, becoming non-existent? The energy by which the water of the sea is constituted, failing to exert itself and the sea disappearing? A shower of rain to-day and no more showers afterward? The effulgence of the sun terminated and no more light or heat?

When we observe that in the kingdom of minerals the divine bounties are continuous, how much more shall we expect and realize in the divine spiritual Kingdom! How much greater the radiation of the lights of God and the bounty of life everlasting upon the soul of man! As the body of the universe is continuous, indestructible, the bounties and bestowals of the divine spirit are everlasting.

I praise God that I am privileged to be present in this revered assembly* which is quickened with spiritual susceptibilities and heavenly attraction; its members investigating the reality; their utmost hope the establishment of international peace and their greatest purpose service to the world of humanity.

When we observe the world of created phenomena we discover that each atom of the atoms of substance is moving through the various degrees and kingdoms of organic life. For instance, consider the ethereal element which is penetrating and traveling through all the contingent realities. When there is vibration or movement in the ethereal element, the eye is affected by that vibration and beholds what is known as light.

In the same manner the bestowals of God are moving and circulating throughout all created things. This illimitable divine bounty has no beginning and will have no ending. It is moving, circulating and becomes effective wherever capacity is developed to receive it. In every station there is a specialized capacity. Therefore we must be hopeful that through the bounty and favor of God, this spirit of life infusing all created things shall quicken humanity and from its bestowals the human world become a divine world, this earthly kingdom the mirror of the realm of divinity, the virtues and perfections of the world of humanity become unveiled and the image and likeness of God be reflected from this temple.

---

*Theosophical Society.

THE LAW OF GOD

SURELY for everything there is an all-comprehending wisdom; especially for the great and important affairs of life. The supreme and most important happening in the human world is the Manifestation of God and the descent of the law of God. The holy, divine Manifestations did not reveal themselves for the purpose of founding a nation, sect or faction. They did not appear in order that a certain number might acknowledge their prophethood. They did not declare their heavenly mission and message in order to lay the foundation for a religious belief. Even His Holiness Christ did not become manifest that we should merely believe in him as the Christ, follow him and adore his mention. All these are limited in scope and requirement whereas the Reality of Christ is an unlimited essence. The infinite and unlimited Reality cannot be bounded by any limitation. Nay, rather His Holiness Christ appeared in order to illumine the world of humanity, to render the earthly world celestial, to make the human kingdom a realm of angels, to unite the hearts, to enkindle the light of love in human souls, so that such souls might become independent, attaining complete unity and fellowship, turning to God, entering into the divine Kingdom, receiving the bounties and bestowals of God and partaking of the manna from heaven. Through Christ they were intended to be baptized by the Holy Spirit, attain a new spirit and realize the life everlasting. All the holy precepts and the announcements of prophetic laws were for these various and heavenly purposes. Therefore we offer thanks to God that although no earthly relation obtains among us, yet—Praise be to God!—ideal and divine bonds blend us together. We have gathered here in this meeting, eagerly anticipating the showing forth of the divine bestowals.

In past centuries the nations of the world have imagined that the law of God demanded blind imitation of ancestral forms of belief and worship. For example the Jews were captives of hereditary racial religious observances. The Mohammedans likewise have been held in the bondage of traditionary forms and ceremonials. The Christians also have been implicit followers of ancient tradition and hereditary teaching. At the same time the basic foundation of the religion of God which was ever the principle of love, unity and the fellowship of humanity has been forsaken and cast aside, each religious system holding tenaciously to imitations of ancestral forms as the supreme essential. Therefore hatred and hostility have appeared in the world instead of the divine fruitage of unity and love. By reason of this it has been impossible for the followers of religion to meet together in fellowship and agreement. Even contact and communication have been considered contaminating and the outcome has been a condition of complete alienation and mutual bigotry. There has been no investigation of the essential underlying basis of reality. One whose father was a Jew, invariably proved to be a Jew; a Mohammedan was born of a Mohammedan; a Buddhist was a Buddhist because of the faith of his father before him; and so on. In brief, religion was a heritage descending from father to son, ancestry to posterity without investigation of the fundamental reality; consequently all religionists were veiled, obscured and at variance.

Praise be to God! We are living in this most radiant century wherein human perceptions have developed and investigations of real foundations characterize mankind. Individually and collectively man is proving and penetrating into the reality of outer and inner conditions. Therefore it has come to pass that we are renouncing all that savors of blind imitation, and impartially and independently investigating truth. Let us understand what constitutes the reality of the divine religions. If a Christian sets aside traditional forms and blind imitation of ceremonials and investigates the reality of the gospels, he will discover that the foundation principles of the teachings of His Holiness Christ were mercy, love, fellowship, benevolence, altruism, the resplendence or radiance of divine bestowals, acquisition of the breaths of the Holy Spirit and oneness with God. Furthermore he will learn that His Holiness declared that the Father "maketh his sun to rise on the evil and on the good and sendeth rain on the just and on the unjust." The meaning of this declaration is that the mercy of God encircles all mankind; that not a single individual is deprived of the mercy of God; and no soul is denied the resplendent bestowals of God. The whole human race is submerged in the sea of the mercy of the Lord and we are all the sheep of the one divine shepherd. Whatever shortcomings exist among us must be remedied. For example those who are ignorant must be educated so that they may become wise; the sick must be treated until they recover; those who are immature must be trained in order to reach maturity; those asleep must be awakened. All this must be accomplished through love and not through hatred and hostility. Furthermore His Holiness Jesus Christ referring to the prophecy of Isaiah, spoke of those who "having eyes, see not, having ears, hear not, having hearts, understand not," yet they were to be healed. Therefore it is evident that the bounties of Christ transformed the eye which was blind into a seeing one, rendered the ear which was formerly deaf, attentive, and made the hard, callous heart tender and sensitive. In other words the meaning is that although the people possess external eyes, yet the insight or perception of the soul is blind; although the outer ear hears, the spiritual hearing is deaf; although they possess conscious hearts they are without illumination; and the bounties of His Holiness Christ save souls from these conditions. It is evident then that the manifestation of the Messiah was synonymous with universal mercy. His providence was universal and his teachings were for all. His lights were not restricted to a few. Every "Christ" came to the world of mankind. Therefore we must investigate the foundation of divine religion, discover its reality, re-establish it and spread its message throughout the world so that it may become the source of illumination and enlightenment to mankind, the spiritually dead become alive, the spiritually blind receive sight and those who are inattentive to God become awakened.

CONTINUITY OF REVELATION

THOSE who are uninformed of the world of reality, who do not comprehend existing things, who are without perception of the inner truth of creation, who do not penetrate the real mysteries of material and spiritual phenomena and who possess only a superficial idea of universal life and being are but embodiments of pure ignorance. They believe only that which they have heard from their fathers and ancestors. Of themselves they have no hearing, no sight, no reason, no intellect; they rely solely upon tradition. Such persons imagine that the dominion of God is an accidental dominion or kingdom.

For instance they believe that this world of existence was created six or seven thousand years ago; as if God did not reign before that time and had no creation before that period. They think that divinity is accidental, for to them divinity is dependent upon existing things whereas in reality as long as there has been a God there has been a creation. As long as there has been light, there have been recipients of that light, for light cannot become manifest unless those things which perceive and appreciate it exist. The world of divinity presupposes creation, presupposes recipients of bounty, presupposes the existence of worlds. No divinity can be conceived as separate from creation, for otherwise it would be like imagining an empire without a people. A king must needs have a kingdom, must needs have an army and subjects. Is it possible to be a king and have no country, no army, no subjects? This is an absurdity. If we say that there was a time when there was no country, no army and no subjects, how then could there have been a king and ruler? For these things are essential to a king.

Consequently just as the reality of divinity never had a beginning, —that is, God has ever been a creator, God has ever been a provider, God has ever been a quickener, God has ever been a bestower,—so there never has been a time when the attributes of God have not had expression. The sun is the sun because of its rays, because of its heat. Were we to conceive of a time when there was a sun without heat and light, it would imply that there had been no sun at all and that it became the sun afterward. So likewise if we say there was a time when God had no creation or created beings, a time when there were no recipients of His bounties and that His names and attributes had not been manifested, this would be equivalent to a complete denial of divinity, for it would mean that divinity is accidental. To explain it still more clearly, if we think that fifty thousand years ago or one hundred thousand years ago there was no creation, that there were then no worlds, no human beings, no animals, this thought of ours would mean that previous to that period there was no divinity. If we should say that there was a time when there was a king but there were no subjects, no army, no country for him to rule over, it would really be asserting that there was a time when no king existed and that the king is accidental. It is therefore evident that inasmuch as the reality of divinity is without a beginning, creation is also without a beginning. This is as clear as the sun. When we contemplate this vast machinery of omnipresent power, perceive this illimitable space and its innumerable worlds it will become evident to us that the life-time of this infinite creation is more than six thousand years; nay, it is very, very ancient.

Notwithstanding this, we read in Genesis in the Old Testament that the lifetime of creation is but six thousand years. This has an inner meaning and significance; it is not to be taken literally. For instance it is said in the Old Testament that certain things were created in the first day. The narrative shows that at that time the sun was not yet created. How could we conceive of a day if no sun existed in the heavens; for the day depends upon the light of the sun? Inasmuch as the sun had not been made, how could the first day be realized? Therefore these statements have significances other than literal.

To be brief; our purpose is to show that the divine sovereignty, the Kingdom of God, is an ancient sovereignty; that it is not an accidental sovereignty; just as a kingdom presupposes the existence of subjects, of an army, of a country; for otherwise the state of dominion, authority and kingdom cannot be conceived of. Therefore if we should imagine that the creation is accidental we would be forced to admit that the creator is accidental whereas the divine bounty is ever flowing and the rays of the Sun of Truth are continuously shining. No cessation is possible to the divine bounty, just as no cessation is possible to the rays of the sun. This is clear and obvious.

Thus there have been many holy Manifestations of God. One thousand years ago, two hundred thousand years ago, one million years ago the bounty of God was flowing, the radiance of God was shining, the dominion of God was existing.

Why do these holy Manifestations of God appear? What is the wisdom and purpose of their coming? What is the outcome of their mission? It is evident that human personality appears in two aspects, —the image or likeness of God and the aspect of Satan. The human reality stands between these two,—the divine and the satanic. It is manifest that beyond this material body, man is endowed with another reality which is the world of exemplars constituting the heavenly body of man. In speaking, man says, "I saw," "I spoke," "I went." Who is this "I"? It is obvious that this "I" is different from this body. It is clear that when man is thinking, it is as though he were consulting with some other person. With whom is he consulting? It is evident that it is another reality or one aside from this body with whom he enters into consultation when he thinks, "Shall I do this work or not?" "What will be the result of my doing this?" Or when he questions the other reality, "What is the objection to this work if I do it?" And then that reality in man communicates its opinion to him concerning the point at issue. Therefore that reality in man is clearly and obviously other than his body, an ego with which man enters into consultation and whose opinion man seeks.

Often a man makes up his mind positively about a matter; for instance he determines to undertake a journey. Then he thinks it over, that is, he consults his inner reality and finally concludes that he will give up his journey. What has happened? Why did he abandon his original purpose? It is evident that he has consulted his inner reality which expresses to him the disadvantages of such a journey, therefore he defers to that reality and changes his original intention.

Furthermore man sees in the world of dreams. He travels in the East, he travels in the West, although his body is stationary, his body is here. It is that reality in him which makes the journey while the body sleeps. There is no doubt that a reality exists other than the outward, physical reality. Again for instance a person is dead, is buried in the ground. Afterward you see him in the world of dreams and speak with him although his body is interred in the earth. Who is the person you see in your dreams, talk to and who also speaks with you? This again proves that there is another reality different from the physical one which dies and is buried. Thus it is certain that in man there is a reality which is not the physical body. Sometimes the body becomes weak but that other reality is in its own normal state. The body goes to sleep, becomes as one dead but that reality is moving about, comprehending things, expressing them and is even conscious of itself.

This other and inner reality is called the heavenly body, the ethereal form which corresponds to this body. This is the conscious reality which discovers the inner meaning of things, for the outer body of man does not discover anything. The inner ethereal reality grasps the mysteries of existence, discovers scientific truths and indicates their technical application. It discovers electricity, produces the telegraph, the telephone and opens the door to the world of arts. If the outer material body did this, the animal would likewise be able to make scientific and wonderful discoveries, for the animal shares with man all physical powers and limitations. What then is that power which penetrates the realities of existence and which is not to be found in the animal? It is the inner reality which comprehends things, throws light upon the mysteries of life and being, discovers the heavenly Kingdom, unseals the mysteries of God and differentiates man from the brute. Of this there can be no doubt.

As we have before indicated, this human reality stands between the higher and the lower in man, between the world of the animal and the world of divinity. When the animal proclivity in man becomes predominant, he sinks even lower than the brute. When the heavenly powers are triumphant in his nature, he becomes the noblest and most superior being in the world of creation. All the imperfections found in the animal are found in man. In him there is antagonism, hatred and selfish struggle for existence; in his nature lurk jealousy, revenge, ferocity, cunning, hypocrisy, greed, injustice and tyranny. So to speak, the reality of man is clad in the outer garment of the animal, the habiliments of the world of nature, the world of darkness, imperfections and unlimited baseness.

On the other hand, we find in him justice, sincerity, faithfulness, knowledge, wisdom, illumination, mercy and pity coupled with intellect, comprehension, the power to grasp the realities of things and the ability to penetrate the truths of existence. All these great perfections are to be found in man. Therefore we say that man is a reality which stands between light and darkness. From this standpoint of view, his nature is threefold, animal, human and divine. The animal nature is darkness; the heavenly is light in light.

The holy Manifestations of God come into the world to dispel the darkness of the animal or physical nature of man, to purify him from his imperfections in order that his heavenly and spiritual nature may become quickened, his divine qualities awakened, his perfections visible, his potential powers revealed and all the virtues of the world of humanity latent within him may come to life. These holy Manifestations of God are the educators and trainers of the world of existence, the teachers of the world of humanity. They liberate man from the darkness of the world of nature, deliver him from despair, error, ignorance, imperfections and all evil qualities. They clothe him in the garment of perfections and exalted virtues. Men are ignorant; the Manifestations of God make them wise. They are animalistic; the Manifestations make them human. They are savage and cruel; the Manifestations lead them into kingdoms of light and love. They are

Pygmy Shrew

Sorex minutus

(Shrew Family)

Identification: HB 4.5-6.5 cm, T 3-4.5 cm, W 3-7 g. Resembles Common Shrew (p. 14) but smaller; snout narrower; tail relatively longer.

Distribution: The whole of Europe except the western Mediterranean and Iceland; temperate parts of Asia to China. Widespread in Britain and Ireland.

Habitat: Woodland edges, hedgerows, damp meadows, gardens, parks; in winter sometimes also in buildings.

Behaviour: Active by night and day; solitary; hunts for food mostly above ground, more rarely in mouse burrows; does not burrow for itself.

Food: Beetles and other insects, spiders, worms, slugs and snails.

Breeding: Mating season Apr-Aug; gestation 19 days; 1-2 litters per year, each with 4-8 young. Development as for Common Shrew.

Shrews are often mistaken for mice, although they are not closely related. Shrews belong to the insectivores, a much older group than the mice in evolutionary terms.

The Pygmy Shrew is one of our smallest mammals. Such very small animals have a high surface area for their overall size and therefore lose a lot of warmth from their bodies. In order to counterbalance this temperature loss they have to take in a lot of energy in the form of food. The Pygmy Shrew begins to starve after only nine hours without food. Every two hours or so they hunt feverishly amongst taller grasses and ground vegetation, taking very short naps between feeding bouts. Like all shrews they do not hibernate, but continue to feed throughout the winter, often underneath the snow.

Alpine Shrew

Sorex alpinus

(Shrew Family)

Identification: HB 6-7.5 cm, T 6-7.5 cm, W 6-10 g. Coat colour slate grey, slightly paler beneath, with whitish feet; snout long and pointed; tail about the same length as the body.

Distribution: Mountains of central Europe, Alps, Pyrenees, Carpathians, Balkans, 500-2500 m.

Habitat: Coniferous woods; damp meadows; mountain streams.

Behaviour: Active by night and day; solitary.

Food: Insects, spiders, woodlice, slugs, snails and worms.

Breeding: Mating season Apr-Aug; breeding biology similar to Common Shrew (p. 14).

This species belongs, with the Pygmy and Common Shrews, to the red-toothed shrew group – the tips of the teeth are dark red. The jaws of shrews are quite different from those of mice. Whereas the rodents have characteristic long, chisel-like cutting teeth at the front of the jaw, a shrew's jaws are more like those of a miniature carnivore, with rows of sharp teeth.

Skull, showing teeth: red-toothed shrew (left), white-toothed shrew (middle), and mouse (right).

Pygmy Shrew (above)
Alpine Shrew (below)

JUST THEN,
I SAW LIGHT.
A WARM,
ENVELOPING
GLOW...

CONTENTS

{ C H A R A C T E R S }

Fuyuki Kanda

The man who lives with Fukumaru. Drawn to Fukumaru from the moment he first laid eyes on the kitty at the pet store, Kanda went on to take Fukumaru home. Kanda was once a celebrated pianist but was unable to return to the stage after his wife's death. He now works as a piano teacher at a music school.

Fukumaru

A cat who lived at the pet store for a long time before Kanda fell in love with him at first sight and adopted him. Fukumaru is an Exotic Shorthair. He adores Kanda, who treasures him, and affectionately calls him "Daddy." He loves food, but he's not so great with baths.

Chako

Natsuhito Kobayashi

Kanda's best friend since early childhood. They're very close, and Kobayashi is always teasing Kanda and cheering him up. He has a Shiba Inu named Chako.

Mrs. Kanda

Kanda's late wife. A great cat lover in life, she inspired her husband to adopt Fukumaru later on.

Momiji Sato

An employee at the pet store where Fukumaru used to live. Worried about Fukumaru because no one wanted to buy him, she always made a point of keeping Fukumaru's spirits up.

Yoshiharu Moriyama

A teacher at the music school where Kanda works. Moriyama also plays in a band, but he keeps that a secret at work. His dream is to hit it big and play concerts at massive venues.

Marin

A female cat once owned by Hibino's mom but since taken in by Hibino himself. She looks just like Fukumaru. As it happens, she is Fukumaru's big sister, and the two are eventually reunited.

Kanade Hibino

A pianist who sees Kanda as his rival. When Hibino's mother forced him to take in her cat, Marin, Hibino reconnected with Kanda. Hibino plays in a band as well.

Music School Staff

The employees at the music school where Kanda and Moriyama work. They secretly idolize Kanda. Mostly women, there are very few men among them.

Masato Moriyama

Yoshiharu Moriyama's little brother and a pupil of Hibino's. The Moriyama brothers have low opinions of each other.

Mom

Mother to both Fukumaru and Marin. Her constant wish is for her children to be happy.

Chapter 57 | Let There Be Mewsic

WANNA START A BAND WITH US?

I'M TELLIN' YA, WE COULD GO PRO!

WHOA! MORIYAMA, MY DUDE! YOU CAN WRITE SONGS?!

YOU'VE GOT A KILLER VOICE!

WE STARTED OUT FOLLOWING THE SAME DREAM.

YOU JUST DON'T HAVE THE TALENT.

YOU KNOW THAT AIN'T GONNA HAPPEN.

HA HA HA! YOU'RE STILL TRYIN' TO MAKE IT BIG?

WHEN DID IT ALL BEGIN TO FALL APART?

WAS IT ALL A LIE?

WHERE IS EVERY-ONE?

WE'RE KEEPING THEM WAITING.

WE'VE GOT AN AUDIENCE.

ARE YOU REALLY GONNA PULL A BRATTY STUNT LIKE THIS AND LEAVE THEM HANGING?

IS THIS IT?

IS THIS WHAT YOU GUYS CALL "FUN"?

GRIP

I'LL SHOW YOU. I'LL SING.

EVEN IF I HAVE TO DO IT ALONE, I'LL SING.

I CAN PLAY MY OWN GUITAR TOO.

I'LL SING. JUST WATCH ME.

...EVERY- THING I'VE BEEN HOLDING IN IS GONNA COME POURING OUT.

IF I FORCE IT...

I GOTTA SING SOON OR ELSE...

CLAMOR CLAMOR CLAMOR CLAMOR

THE CROWD'S GROWING REST- LESS.

STAMP

IT'LL ALL SPILL OUT...

I CAN'T.

SING.

SING.

C'MON, MAN. I'M BEGGIN' YOU...

YOU BET I AM.

RIGHT ON! YOU SURE YOU'RE UP FOR THIS?

YOU CAN COUNT ME IN TOO.

LET ME AT THOSE KEYS.

ALL RIGHT.

LET'S BEGIN, SHALL WE?

MY COLLEAGUE, TAKASHI KAGENAKA.

HE'S A GREAT DRUMMER!

WHO IS THIS GUY?

SMAS-SH

WOOHOO!

MOI WILL PLAY TOO-HOO!

MR. KAGENAKA! I DIDN'T KNOW YOU WERE HERE!

BOING

IF WE START TO PLAY, AND IT BEGINS TO FEEL LIKE ONE OF YOUR CONCERTS...

MR. KANDA!

YOU CAN'T GET UP ONSTAGE, REMEM-BER?!

...YOU COULD COL-LAPSE!

WHY WOULD YOU RISK GETTING HURT...

...FOR A NOBODY LIKE ME?

WHY WOULD YOU PUSH YOURSELF LIKE THIS?

THANK YOU FOR STEPPING UP.

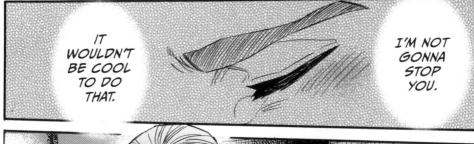

IT WOULDN'T BE COOL TO DO THAT.

I'M NOT GONNA STOP YOU.

I'LL TAKE A PAGE OUT OF YOUR BOOK...

...AND SUCK IT UP.

...BECAUSE I'M PLAYING FOR MY FRIEND.

I CAN STAND HERE NOW...

IT'S JUST LIKE...

...WHEN I PLAYED FOR YOU...

HE SAID HE'S JUST BEEN TEACHING LITTLE KIDS ALL THIS TIME, BUT THAT'S GOTTA BE A LIE.

IF THAT'S TRUE, HOW IS HE NOT RUSTY?!

TOO GOOD!!

OF COURSE KANDA'S FREAKY GOOD!!

Chapter 58 Fukumaru & His Merry Pals

I HATE YOUR TALENT!!

I HATE IT!!

IS HE JUST THAT MUCH MORE TALENTED THAN I AM?!

KANDA.

I'M SURE YOU'RE PUSHING YOURSELF HARD.

UGH!

THAT TOTALLY MESSES WITH MY HEAD.

I BET THIS ISN'T EVEN CLOSE TO HIS USUAL.

Chapter 58 | Fukumaru & His Merry Pals

THANK YOU SO MUCH.

THANK YOU FOR PLAYING ALL THE WAY TO THE END.

IT'S ALL THANKS TO YOU, MR. KANDA.

BECAUSE YOU JOINED ME UP THERE...

...I WAS ABLE TO SING.

THAT WAS THE BEST SHOW EVER.

MR. KAGE-NAKA.

MR. HIBINO.

AND I WAS ABLE TO STAND ONSTAGE BECAUSE OF YOU. ALL OF YOU.

MISS SATO.

KO-BAYASHI.

FUKU-MARU.

IT WOULD HAVE BEEN IMPOSSIBLE ON MY OWN.

...AT THAT MOMENT...

...I WAS ABLE TO GET ON THAT STAGE WITHOUT A SECOND THOUGHT.

AND YOU, MR. MORIYAMA. BECAUSE YOU WERE THERE...

ROCK ON!!

HEY, GANG !!

IT'S AFTER-PARTY TIIIIME !!

I'M WORRIED ABOUT FUKUMARU.

FRET あせ FRET あせ

I'M GOING HOME.

MOI WILL COME ALONG TOO-HOO!

MR. KANDA. WE'LL SEE YOU HOME.

SO WOULD I.

MAY I GO WITH YOU?

I'D LIKE TO SEE HIM.

MERRY わい MERRY わい

MERRY わい MERRY わい

AWRIGHT!!

AFTERPARTY AT KANDA'S!!

IT'LL BE AN AFTER-PARTY WHERE WE ADMIRE LI'L FUKU ALL QUIET, LIKE.

OKAY, OKAY, GEEZ!

HNRRGH...

YOU MUSTN'T BE NOISY. YOU'LL SCARE FUKUMARU.

IS HE BEIN' A GOOD BOY?

I WONDER HOW THE LI'L GUY'S DOING.

IS HE TUCKERED OUT AND FAST ASLEEP?

URP!

I'M SO SMART.

WHAT A GREAT FIND.

NOM NOM NOM

A BAG THAT GIVES MEW FOOD.

I'M LONELY ...

I WONDER WHAT HE'S DOING.

I HOPE HE COMES HOME SOON.

WHEN WILL DADDY BE BACK?

MUNCH MUNCH

CLACK
カッ
カッ

BUT...

...FUR SOME REASON...

I HEAR DADDY'S FOOT-STEPS!!

ダッ ダッ ダッ ダッ
DASH DASH DASH

...I HEAR OTHER FOOTSTEPS TOO...

ぞ"3
CROWD

JUST LOOK HOW THIN HE IS!

LI'L FUKU'S ALL SKIN AND BONES?!

LOTS AND LOTS OF THEM!!

SKINNY-MARU-HOO!

I'M HOME, FUKU-MARU.

FUKU-MARU, ARE YOU OKAY?!

CROWD
ぞ"3

FUKU-MARU.

FUKU-MARU.

LITTLE FUKU-MARU.

I GUESS YOU WOULDN'T, HUH?

DO YOU RE-MEMBER ME?

I RE-MEMBER MEW.

MRR, MRR, MEEEOW!

MEW'RE...

...WHO WAS ALWAYS NICE TO ME...

...THE LADY FROM THE PET SHOP...

PURR PURR PURR PURR PURR

HE'S TOO PRECIOUS. I CAN'T LET HIM GO.

SHALL I TAKE HIM FOR YOU?

YOUR LEGS MUST BE FALLING ASLEEP.

PLEASE LET ME HOLD HIM A LITTLE LONGER.

I NEVER THOUGHT I'D GET TO PET HIM AGAIN.

IT REALLY BURNS ME UP.

IRK IRK イラ イラ

WHAT'S WITH THE ATMO-SPHERE?

?

DON'T BOTHER COMING BACK... ...KANDA.

IRK IRK イラ イラ

YOU REALLY ARE MY NEMESIS.

HUH?

BADUMP

WELL, I FELL HEAD OVER HEELS FOR HIBINON'S GUITAR!

HEY, YOU KANDA-CULTIST, I AIN'T YOUR YES-MAN.

HOW CAN I DISAGREE NOW?

MR. HIBINO!

WASN'T MR. KANDA JUST THE BEST?!

ムギーッ FUME

I, ERM...

HM?

COMPLIMENTS FROM THIS GUY JUST DON'T MAKE ME HAPPY.

GUITARS REALLY ARE JUST SO COOL! ALL THAT "SCREEEE" AND "NYEOOOOW"!

YIKES...

HUH?

MAYBE I SHOULD TAKE UP THE GUITAR TOO...

SHOCKED
ガーン

FUYUKI KANDA IS JEALOUS OF MEEE ?!

NAH, DON'T. IT'S NOT YOUR THING.

WHY NOT ?!

DON'T TELL ME KANDA'S JEALOUS?

IS IT 'COS THE GORILLA COMPLI-MENTED ME?!

SAY WHAT ?!

UH, GUH, GUH, GUH!

I BEAT HIM!! I BESTED KANDA- AAAA!!

I'M ON TOP OF THE WORLD !!

BEING HAPPY MAKES ME WANNA PET CATS.

HEY, LI'L FUKU! WHAT A GOOD LI'L GUY.

ISN'T HE, MR. KAGE- NAKA?! ISN'T HE JUST?

MY, HE'S A CUTIE PATOO- TIE!

FUKU- MARU IS ADOR- ABLE!

PURR PURR PURR

ALLOW MOI TO PET HIM TOO- HOO.

OH, FINE. IF I MUST.

TAKE IT EASY WITH HIM.

IT'S KINDA LIVELY AROUND HERE.

Chapter 59 | Dad's Voice

HA HA HA!

ず"___GLUM ん....

THE GATE JUST WASN'T TALL ENOUGH...

'COURSE NOT! HE'S A CAT!

I DECIDED TO TRY ATTENDING ANOTHER PIANO CONCERT.

HEY, IT'S GETTIN' TO BE THAT TIME.

I THINK I CAN MANAGE IT NOW.

WELL, UNLIKE BEFORE, I SHOULD BE ABLE TO SIT THROUGH IT AT LEAST.

COME ON.

...OR NOT.

DO YOU HATE MY CONCERTS THAT MUCH?!!

BAM

MR. KANDA! YOU LEFT IN THE MIDDLE AGAIN!

AND IT ISN'T RUDE TO ME?!

...WE THOUGHT IT WOULD BE RUDE TO THE OTHER AUDIENCE MEMBERS IF WE—

WELL, SINCE LEAVING OUR SEATS WAS A DISTINCT POSSI-BILITY...

ANSWER MY QUES-TION!

MR. HIBINO HAS VERY GOOD EYES!

GOOD JOB NOTICING WE WERE IN THE LAST ROW.

RAWR

DON'T GO ASSUMING THAT TERM EXCUSES ANYTHING AND EVERY-THING!

GRAWR

DON'T GET SO TETCHY, HIBINON. WE'RE FRIENDS, AIN'T WE?!

...WE'RE HERE FOR YA.

IT GOES BOTH WAYS, HIBINON. IF SOMETHING'S ON YOUR MIND OR YOU'RE IN TROUBLE...

WHILE I'VE GIVEN A LOT OF THOUGHT TO MY OPTIONS...

THE THING IS...

I DON'T NEED YOU FOR ANYTHING, MR. NATSU-HITO...

...BUT THERE IS SOME-THING I'D LIKE TO ASK MR. KANDA.

HUH? YOU DON'T NEED ME?

MR. KANDA.

YOU SEE...

BUT I DO REALIZE THAT WHAT I'M ABOUT TO ASK OF YOU IS AN INCONVE-NIENCE, SO FEEL FREE TO REFUSE.

...THEY'D BE TOO HARD ON MARIN FOR ANY LENGTH OF TIME...

THANK YOU SO MUCH!

OH! FUKU-MARU'S HERE.

PRR! MROWR!

PRR! MEW!

HEY! SIS IS HERE.

MEOW!

MEOW!

MEOW!

TIME TO PLAAAY!

...SHE WON'T HAVE FORGOTTEN ME, WILL SHE?

IT'S GOING TO BE FINE.

WHEN I GET BACK...

THEY REALLY DO.

MEOW!

MEOW!

THEY GET ALONG WELL, DON'T THEY?

THE LITTLE GUY'S ALREADY BACK TO NORMAL.

CAN YOU SEE ME?

HEY, MARIN!

MARIN, IT'S ME!

SEE, MARIN...

MARIN, TODAY, I'M...

SO DON'T WORRY, ALL RIGHT?

I'LL BE BACK SOON, OKAY?

ARE YOU BEING A GOOD GIRL?

I'M NOT SURE MARIN REGISTERED THAT IT WAS HER PERSON'S VOICE.

BUT UNTIL THE VIDEO ENDED...

...MARIN WAS GLUED TO THAT SPOT.

WAGGLE
WAGGLE

WHAT DO YOU THINK?

NATURE'S VERY OWN CAT TEASERS. I PRESENTED FUKUMARU WITH ONE.

GREEN FOXTAIL (SETARIA VIRIDIS).

SHABAR

BAP

BAP BAP

BAP

HE'S THREE TIMES MORE EAGER THAN NORMAL!!

ONLY ...

ONLY ...

SNAP

SNAP

SNAP

SNAP

SNAP

SNAP

I NEVER IMAGINED HE'D BE THIS HAPPY!

WILD CAT TEASERS ARE JUST INCRED-IBLE!

SNAP

BUT THE MAN CONTINUED TO PICK CAT TEASERS WHENEVER HE SAW THEM.

ALL IN PIECES
ばらばらーん

...THEY'RE FAR TOO FRAGILE...

LOVEY-DOVEY COUPLE

THE CAT TEASERS ARE GONE!!

THEY'RE GONE!!

WAS IT A THIEF?!

THEY WERE JUST HERE!

WHERE DID THEY GO?!

PANIC あわ
PANIC あわ

A THIEF. YES...

OVERSEAS...

WHENEVER I LAND IN ANOTHER COUNTRY...

...MY HEART RACES...

MEOW!

...BUT I MISS MARIN LIKE CRAZY RIGHT NOW!!

MRR, MRR, MRR, MRR!

WAAAH!

HOW AM I SUPPOSED TO LIVE WITHOUT HER FOR TWO WHOLE WEEKS?!

MARIIIIN!

I'LL DO MY BEST!!

...DADDY!

I'LL GET DADDY TO PET ME A WHOLE BUNCH AGAIN TODAY.

TMP TMP TMP TMP
た た た た た

THEN I'LL FALL FAST ASLEEP ON HIS LAP.

WHERE ARE MEW?

PEEK
キョろ

PEEK
キョろ

DADDY! DADDY!

POKE
つんつん

ARE MEW IN HERE?

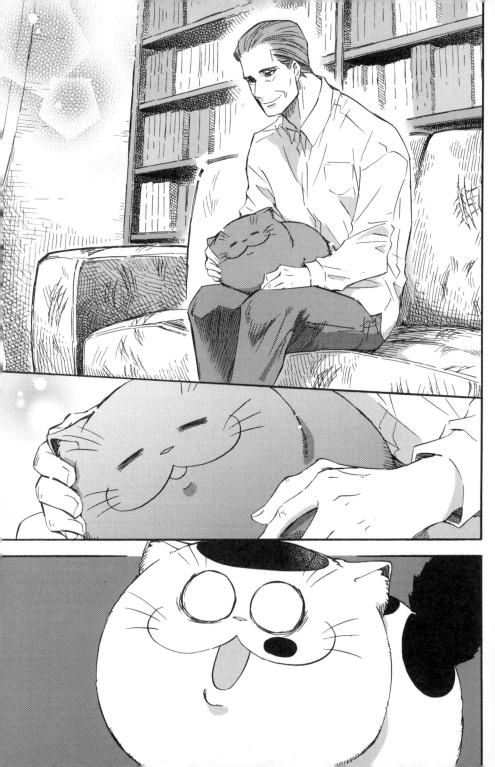

HOW CUTE ARE THEY?!

TA-DA

POOR YOU-HOO! AND YOUR BLADDER...

IT WAS TWO HOURS BEFORE THEY DECIDED TO GET DOWN, SO I DIDN'T MOVE A MUSCLE.

I COULDN'T AGREE MORE! THEY'RE JUST TOO SWEET.

WHAT BLISS!

THEY BOTH CLIMBED INTO MY LAP YESTERDAY!

HERE, LOOK AT THIS! SEE?

MERRY

MERRY

HEH HEH HEH!

OH, MR. MORI-YAMA, NO...

BY THE WAY, MR. MORIYAMA ISN'T HERE YET, IS HE?

WANTS TO SHOW OFF...

I'M ACTUALLY CAT-SITTING FOR A FRIEND.

YOU HAVE TWO CATS, MR. KANDA?

HE'S OUT SICK WITH A FEVER.

WATER
...

WATER
...

I'M COLD
...

AND I'VE GOT A ROARING HEADACHE.

FLUMPPP....

CAN'T MOVE...

MUSIC

SHE MIGHT BE HOME. MAYBE I SHOULD CALL THE HOUSE.

...WITH NO LUCK.

I'VE TRIED CALLING A BUNCH OF TIMES...

MOM'S THE TYPE WHO NEVER HAS HER PHONE ON HER...

DAD'S AT WORK.

KACHAK

IT'LL PROLLY BE OKAY.

HE HATES PHONES.

IT'D BE AWKWARD IF MY KID BROTHER ANSWERED, THOUGH.

WELL...

MUSIC

IT'S HIM!!

YES, MORIYAMA RESIDENCE.

WHERE ARE MOM AND DAD AT?

HOW RANDOM. WHAT DO YOU WANT?

YOSHI-HARU?

HA -HA -HA...

UH, HEY, MASATO.

I'VE GOT A FEVER, AND I CAN'T MOVE!

HEY!! LOOK, I'M SORRY TO ASK, BUT—!!

COULD YOU PICK UP MEDS, DRINKS, AND FOOD FOR ME?

WORK.

THAT DELIGHTED FACE MUST'VE GOTTEN UNDER MY SKIN.

WATCH ME, YOSH!

LOOK, LOOK!

I WONDER WHY I COULDN'T JUST GENUINELY CHEER HIM ON.

...IS THE SAME AS WHAT THEY DID TO ME...

WHAT I DID TO YOU...

I'M SORRY, MASATO...

I'M DONE RUNNING.

NEVER AGAIN!

SOME-ONE...

...WHO CAN ACCEPT BOTH JOY AND SADNESS...

I WANT TO BE MORE LIKE MR. KANDA.

BUT...

UH, HUUUH?!

WOULD YOU SIGN WITH US FOR YOUR DEBUT?

I SAW YOUR GIG ON SATURDAY.

AND TO TOP IT ALL OFF, YOU HAD THE SONGS TO BACK IT UP. THEY'RE TERRIFIC.

I HAVEN'T BEEN THAT MOVED IN AGES.

...AND ROCKING OUT ON THAT STAGE.

YOU WERE AWESOME, RALLYING WITH THE HELP OF SUCH INSPIRING FRIENDS...

ABSO-LUTELY.

BUT I DO HAVE ONE CONDI-TION.

FOR REAL?!

I THINK YOU CAN BE A STAR.

MR. MORI-YAMA?

IT'S ME, KANDA.

ARE YOU FEELING BETTER?

Chapter 61 | A Warm Flavor

M-MR. KANDA...

JUMP

MR. MORI-YAMA?

ARE YOU ALL RIGHT?

...IS AT MY FRONT DOOR!!

J-JUST A MINUTE!

PANIC PANIC

NO WAY! DID HE COME HERE OUT OF WORRY FOR ME?!

STOMP

THUMP

MR. MORI-YAMA.

ONE SEC!

STOMP

MR. MORI-YAMA.

WHUMP

NEARLY DONE!

MR. MORI-YAMA.

SORRY TO KEEP YOU WAIT-ING!

THUMP

LEMME CLEAN UP A LI'L!

MY PLACE IS A WRECK!!

MESSY

MR. MORI-YAMA...

...IS SO NICE.

MR. KANDA...

WE'RE GOING TO THE HOSPITAL.

THAT'S WHY I END UP THINKING AWFUL THINGS.

LIKE, "IF I CRIED AND BEGGED HIM TO FORM A BAND WITH ME...

"...HE'D PROBABLY AGREE."

OH DEAR... DO YOU NOT LIKE IT?!

WHAT'S WRONG?!

FRET

FRET あわわ

NO, IT'S REALLY GOOD.

うぐっ

GNRGH!

WHAT A NASTY LINE OF THOUGHT, YOSHI-HARU!!!

MADE FROM LEFTOVERS

THANK YOU SO MUCH! THIS IS ONE OF MY FAVORITE THINGS TO EAT.

WHO'D HAVE THOUGHT YOU COULD MAKE SOMETHING THIS TASTY FROM THE STUFF RATTLING AROUND MY BARE FRIDGE?

FLUFFY EGG & RICE PORRIDGE

...BUT FOR SOME REA-SON...

...SO I ASKED HER TO TEACH ME HOW TO MAKE IT...

IT WAS DELI-CIOUS...

MY WIFE OFTEN COOKED IT FOR ME WHEN I DIDN'T HAVE MUCH OF AN APPETITE.

THE KEY TO EGG & RICE PORRIDGE IS ADDING A LITTLE MISO PASTE!

HUH!

...IT NEVER TASTES THE WAY HERS DID.

NO, NO. PLEASE DON'T WORRY ABOUT IT!

FRET FRET あせあせ

I'M SORRY FOR BRINGING UP SOMETHING MELANCHOLY.

AND THAT'S WHY THE TASTE OF THIS TO ME NOW...

...MIGHT BE THE SAME AS WHAT YOU TASTED WHEN SHE'D MAKE THIS FOR YOU.

I BET HER LOVE GAVE THAT SPECIAL SOMETHING.

...YEAH, BEST TURN THAT OFFER DOWN.

I WILL!

THERE'S STILL PLENTY MORE.

EAT UP, NOW!

I CAN'T DRAG MR. KANDA INTO THIS.

THANK YOU!

THIS IS TOO-HOO GOOD!

...TO FIGHT MY WAY UP.

I'LL DO EVERY-THING IN MY POWER...

YOU STAY RIGHT WHERE YOU ARE, MR. MORIYAMA.

I'LL ANSWER IT.

WHO COULD THAT BE?

A SALES-PERSON, MAYBE...?

OH, THANK YOU.

DING-DOOONG ピンポーン

JUST A MINUTE!

MY APOLOGIES FOR THE DELAY.

CLACK ガッ×

HUH ?!

GOD ?!

K-KA...

G-G-GUH...

ERM...

MAY I HELP YOU?

FUKUMARU COMES WHEN I CALL.

COME HERE.

OVER HERE.

FUKU-MARU!

NO...

THAT'S NOT WHAT I MEANT.

WAGGLE WAGGLE
フリフリ

WAGGLE WAGGLE WAGGLE WAGGLE
フリフリ フリフリ

SHF SHF SHF

SEE? FUKUMARU DOES COME WHEN I CALL.

I REELED HIM IN!

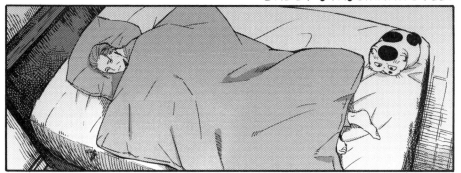

OWW!!

CHOMP

IF I PULL MY FEET IN, THOUGH, I'LL BE FINE...

HEH HEH! WHAT WILL WE DO WITH YOU, HM?

SHWIP

FUKU-MARU IS A CLEVER CAT.

OR NOT!!

CHOMP

CHOMP

CHOMP

ZWOOP

THIS IS MY FAVORITE BOX.

GNAW GNAW

THIS IS ALSO MY FAVORITE BOX.

GNAW GNAW

AND THIS ONE.

SO'S THIS ONE.

AND THIS.

THIS ONE TOO.

HEAPED

すっら〜〜ん

PTOOEY!

PTOOEY!

FUKUMARU CONTINUES ACQUIRING MORE HOUSES.

I CAN'T THROW THEM AWAY...

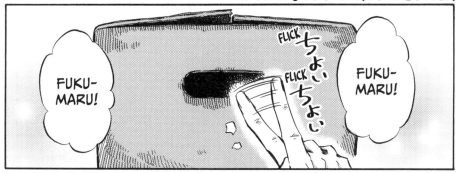

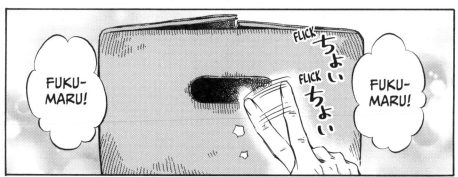

Meowy
Bedfellows

SHE'S GETTING CLOSER AND CLOSER...!

OH, HOW WONDERFUL!

YOU'RE GOING TO SLEEP WITH US TOO, MARIN?

MUH-MROWR?!

...FELL ASLEEP WITH HIS FACE TURNED TOWARD SIS...

DADDY...

AS LONG AS I CAN BE NEAR DADDY...

...A CORNER'S ENOUGH FUR ME.

I'M OKAY IN THE CORNER HERE...

IT'S FINE. I'LL GET OVER IT.

SIS CAN HAVE MEOWY SPOT BY DADDY'S FACE.

WHY?

S-SIS...

...WANT TO BE CLOSE TO ME?

IT WASN'T DADDY SHE WAS AFTER...

SIS... DID MEW MAYBE...

Chapter 62 | **Sibling Harmeowny**

THIS PLACE SURE IS WILD!

WHAT'S TAINTED IS YOUR BRAIN!!!

MR. KANDA HAS BEEN TAIIINTED!

OH, I HAD NO IDEA!

WE WORK AT THE SAME MUSIC SCHOOL, YOU SEE.

YOU EVEN GOT ME MEDICINE...

BUT I'M SURPRISED YOU CAME BY, LI'L BRO.

BECAUSE I HAD A FEELING THIS'D HAPPEN!!

WHY DIDN'T MY STUPID BROTHER MENTION THAT?

THANKS, MASATO.

THAT MAKES ME HAPPY.

WHY WOULD YOU SAY THAT?

DID YOU EAT SOMETHING WEIRD?

ALL I DID WAS ENVY HIS CHOPS.

I WAS A LOUSY BIG BROTHER.

IS THAT TRUE?

Y- YES.

WHEN WE WERE KIDS, HE WAS COLD TO ME AND PUSHED ME AWAY BECAUSE HE WAS JEALOUS OF MY TALENT FOR THE PIANO.

MR. KANDA, LISTEN.

THIS GUY'S AN AWFUL BIG BROTHER.

WAH, WAH, WAH! STOP!

I LIKE YOUR SOUND.

MY LITTLE BROTHER...

...IS STILL A GOOD KID.

IT'S FROM MY FRIEND, SOTA.

HUH?

...YOUR BROTHER...

ISN'T THAT...

...AND FUYUKI KANDA?!!

WHAT DO YOU WANT, SOTA?!

I'M IN THE MIDDLE OF SOMETHING GOOD.

MASATO!

CHECK OUT THE VIDEO LINK I SENT YOU RIGHT NOW!

Death by
Flattery

NO WAAAY...

SEEMS HE WANTS TO PRIORITIZE HIS TIME WITH HIS FAMILY!

THAT'S RIGHT.

MR. KANDA DOESN'T TAKE STUDENTS?!

FWIP

SHOCKED

...SQUASHED.

MY DREAM OF STUDYING UNDER MR. KANDA...

ALL THE BIG PIANISTS MUST BE ACQUAINTED WITH MR. KANDA.

I'LL GET ONE OF THEM TO TAKE ME ON AS A PUPIL, THEN WAIT FOR MY CHANCE!

CLENCH

AS IF I'D GIVE UP!!

KANDA?

I HATE THAT GUY.

HUH?

ARE YOU A KANDA FAN TOO?

MASATO, DON'T TELL ME...

I PICKED THE LEAST COMPATIBLE ONNNE!!

I MESSED UUUP!!

I BLEW IIIIIIT!!

WA A A AAUGH!

I MOVED UP IN THIS WORLD BECAUSE I IDOLIZED YOU.

YOU ARE MY ONE AND ONLY SUN, MR. HIBINO.

NO OTHER PIANIST CAN SURPASS YOU.

MR. HIBINO, YOU'RE MY EVERY-THING.

TO THAT END, NO MATTER HOW ROCKY THE PATH MAY BE, I'LL FORGE AHEAD!!

IT'S MY DREAM TO JOIN YOU ONSTAGE ONE DAY.

I WANT TO ACQUIRE THE SKILLS THAT WILL ALLOW ME TO STAND BESIDE YOU.

HM? WHAT DO YOU MEAN?

HEY, MASATO?

THE DEATH BY FLATTERY TECHNIQUE DOES HAVE A SIDE EFFECT.

I HEARD HE WAS REAL STRICT, AND HIS STUDENTS KEEP GETTING DISCOURAGED.

ARE YOU DOING OKAY WITH MR. HIBINO'S LESSONS?

THOSE PEOPLE ARE JUST LOOKING FOR SOMEONE ELSE TO BLAME FOR THEIR OWN FAILURES!

WHO TOLD YOU THAT?

HUNH?!

BESIDES, HIS PIANO SKILLS ARE JUST SHORT OF MR. KANDA'S.

MR. HIBINO'S A GOOD TEACHER.

TAKASHI KAGENAKA

BIRTHDAY: MARCH 19
HEIGHT: 177CM (APPROX. 5'10")
FAVORITE FOOD: CURRY RICE

KANDA'S COLLEAGUE.
DESPITE HIS STRIKING PERSONALITY, HE'S
GREAT AT BLENDING INTO THE SHADOWS.
ALTHOUGH HE'S PARTICULARLY SKILLED ON
THE DRUMS, HE'S AN ALL-ROUNDER WHO
CAN PLAY THE GUITAR AND PIANO TOO.
HE SECRETLY ADMIRES MR. KANDA GREATLY
BECAUSE HE'LL CASUALLY STRIKE UP
CONVERSATIONS.
HE HAS A CUTE GIRLFRIEND.

MASATO MORIYAMA

BIRTHDAY: MARCH 6
HEIGHT: 170CM (APPROX. 5'7")
FAVORITE FOOD: PANCAKES, STRAWBERRIES

YOSHIHARU MORIYAMA'S LITTLE BROTHER.
KANADE HIBINO'S PUPIL.
HIS PIANO SKILLS ARE BETTER THAN HIS BIG
BROTHER'S, BUT HE'S AWARE THAT THERE IS
MORE TO TALENT. TO ACHIEVE HIS DREAMS,
HE'LL PLAY THE HYPOCRITE WHENEVER NECESSARY.
HOWEVER, HE IDOLIZES MR. KANDA AND ALWAYS
ENDS UP SHOWING HIS TRUE COLORS IN HIS
HERO'S PRESENCE.
KANDA CULTIST.

SOTA KAZAMA

BIRTHDAY: OCTOBER 1
HEIGHT: 169CM (APPROX. 5'6½")
FAVORITE FOOD: SALMON RICE BALLS,
⠀⠀⠀⠀⠀⠀⠀⠀⠀⠀⠀⠀⠀DRIED, SEASONED SEAWEED

MASATO MORIYAMA'S FRIEND.
HE'S PRETTY SKILLED AT THE PIANO, BUT HE'S THE
TYPE WHO CAN'T PLAY HIS BEST UNDER PRESSURE.
JUST LIKE MASATO, HE WORSHIPS MR. KANDA.
HE HAS A PET HAMSTER.

WHEN SUMMER CAME...

...FUKUMARU STOPPED SLEEPING WITH ME.

ZZZ... ZZZ...

...I CAN JUST GO TO HIM.

IF FUKUMARU WON'T COME TO ME...

CLING

GO ON.

PAT

FUKU-MARU. YOU CAN LIE ON THIS. IT'S COOL.

ONE HOT SUMMER DAY, I BOUGHT AN ALUMINUM SHEET FOR FUKUMARU.

TMP TMP TMP TMP TMP

ZZZ...

ZZZ...

FLOP

EVEN SO, I'LL KEEP BUYING.

I KNEW IT.

Chapter 63 | **Daddy of the Big Four**

...I GET THE FEELING MY PERFORMANCES ARE LESS HESITANT.

THEY SEEM TO SPARKLE AND SHINE.

EVER SINCE MARIN CAME TO LIVE WITH ME...

MY SOLE COMFORT...

...IS THE PHOTOS AND VIDEOS KANDA SENDS DAILY.

I'M LONELY.

BUT NOW I'M OVER-SEAS...

...FAR AWAY FROM MARIN...

HEY.

HM?

LI'L FUKU'S PRETTY CUTE TOO...

MARIN IS ULTRA CUTE!

HAVE I GOTTEN A LITTLE CLOSER TO HIM?

AAAAAAH! I LOVE YOU!!

IT WAS GOOD, HUH?

YEAH. I'M GLAD I CAME.

SO HIBINO'S CONCERT...

MEN ON THE STREET?

OR IS HE STILL FAR AWAY ON THE HORIZON?

ACCORDING TO HIBINO.

IN PRACTICAL TERMS, I'M JAPAN'S TOP PIANIST!!

AND ANYWAY, THAT GUY'S AWOL.

I KNEW IT! I'M AWESOME!!

YES?

HIBINO.

GO THOOM

GO THOOM

GO THOOM

I'LL KEEP GOING AND THRASH THE WORLD'S GREATEST PIANISTS TOO!!

...THERE ARE FOUR RENOWNED PIANISTS...

...WHO REIGN AT THE TOP.

GLOBALLY SPEAKING...

HE DOESN'T LIKE ANIMALS.

GUSTAVE LAMBERT.

CAT PERSON.

MARGARETHE DRESSEL.

PROBABLY A DOG PERSON.

SILVERT KAMINSKI.

ABSOLUTE CAT FIEND.

AND FUYUKI KANDA, WHO'S CURRENTLY MIA.

GEOFFROY LAMBERT.

HE HATES ANIMALS.

THIS MAN...

...IS GUSTAVE'S SON.

I HAVE A QUESTION FOR YOU.

NOBODY ASKED.

I'M A CAT PERSON.

I'M NOT GREAT WITH THIS GUY.

THEY ARE, HUH?

...BUT THE PEOPLE AROUND YOU ARE ONTO YOU.

YOU FEIGN OTHERWISE...

YOU'RE AS CRASS AS EVER, I SEE.

PLEASE LET ME BE YOUR PUPIL!!

I'M KANADE HIBINO! I'M HERE FROM JAPAN.

WHO ARE YOU?

...IN MY EAGERNESS TO BEST KANDA.

BACK IN MIDDLE SCHOOL, I VISITED GUSTAVE...

BEGGING YOUR PARDON!

WITHOUT AN APPOINTMENT, OF COURSE.

CLACK

KNOCK

KNOCK

KNOCK

Chapter 64 | Go Fur It, Mori-Mori

THAT WAS WHAT MY TEACHER, KANADE HIBINO, TOLD ME.

ALWAYS KEEP YOUR COOL.

...PIANISTS HAVE TO GIVE THE AUDIENCE THEIR BEST PERFORMANCE.

REGARDLESS OF THE VENUE...

...OR WHAT ACCIDENTS HAPPEN...

NO MATTER WHAT HAPPENS...

...KEEP CALM, DON'T RUSH...

YOU LEARN BY MAKING A HABIT OF STAYING COOL AT ALL TIMES.

JUST STAYING ALERT DURING CONCERTS...

...WON'T HELP YOU LEARN TO COPE WITH SUDDEN SITUATIONS.

YES, SIR!!

...AND DEAL WITH IT, MORIYAMA.

AS IF I COULD STAY CALM!!

WHY ARE MY BROTHER AND MR. KANDA IN A BAND TO-GETHER?!

DIDN'T YOU SAY YOU HATED MR. KANDA?

AND ACTUALLY, NOW THAT I'M LOOKING, MR. HIBINO'S THERE TOO!!

WAAAAAH!

LET ME IN TOOOOOO!!

TELL MEEEEE!!

WHEN DID YOU GET TO KNOW EACH OTHER?!

JUST LOOK AT THIS!!

SO MANY PEOPLE ARE LISTENING!!

WELL, IT'S A GOOD SONG!!

LET'S UPLOAD THE NEXT ONE TOO!!

OF COURSE THEY'D LISTEN!!

...IT HAS ALL THOSE VIEWS...

BE-SIDES...

I KNOW. YOU'RE TOO KIND, MR. MORI-YAMA.

NO, I—!

...BECAUSE YOU'RE IN IT, MR. KANDA!

I'M NOT THE ONE WHO POSTED THAT...

THAT MAY BE TRUE...

...BUT AS LONG AS THEY LISTEN TO THE MUSIC, IT DOESN'T MATTER.

HEH HEH!

...BECAUSE NO ONE LISTENED TO THEM.

...SIMPLY DISAPPEAR...

I'VE SEEN MANY TALENTED PEOPLE...

PEOPLE ALWAYS SAID MY MUSIC ONLY SOLD BECAUSE I WAS HANDSOME.

URK!

SAID IT TOO.

Y-YES.

YOU'RE BEAUTIFUL!

I'M LOOKING SHARP, AREN'T I?

GIVE IT YOUR BEST, MR. MORIYAMA.

AND...I'M SORRY.

I'M SURE I'M THE CAUSE OF YOUR WORRIES.

YES?

SAKUMA HERE.

VRRR

VRRR

WELL, I DO HAVE A CAT NOW!

MROWR!

Chapter 65 | Mew're a Daddy's Boy

...I'VE BEEN DOING REALLY WELL.

SINCE KANDA VANISHED...

DON'T TELL ME HE'S MAKING A COMEBACK.

HUNH?! YOU'RE ACTUALLY GONNA DO IT?!

I'LL ASK KANDA.

ALL RIGHT.

HOW SHOULD I KNOW?

JUST ASK HIM YOUR-SELF.

WHAT'S WRONG WITH YOU?!!

SERI-OUSLY?! DON'T! WHAT'S THE POINT OF ASKING ABOUT THAT?!

I HEARD ABOUT THAT VIDEO...

WHAT'S GOING ON?!

...FROM MY FATHER.

MY FATHER CALLED ME.

...YESTERDAY AFTER MY CONCERT.

IT WAS...

I THOUGHT THAT THE TIME HAD COME AND HE'D FINALLY ACKNOWLEDGE ME.

BUT I STILL GOT MY HOPES UP.

HE'S NEVER HAD ANYTHING NICE TO SAY ABOUT MY PERFORMANCES...

AS I TOOK THE CALL, I WAS TREMBLING WITH JOY.

...OR EXPRESSED HIS APPRECIATION AFTER.

HE HAS A CONCERT...

...THERE IS ONLY MUSIC.

IN MY FATHER'S WORLD...

...DIDN'T I REALIZE IT SOONER?

WHY...

KANA-DE...

YOU KNOW KANDA, DON'T YOU?

YES, OF COURSE.

NOW I'VE GOT IT.

I CAN'T WAIT TO HEAR KANDA PLAY AGAIN...

A Man and His Cat ⑥ – THE END

MROWR!

HEY! CAN'T WAIT FOR THAT!

...BUT THERE'S GOING TO BE A NEW CAT IN VOLUME 7!

THE MAN'S WILD CONCERT, THE MORIYAMA BROTHERS, AND A MYSTERY MAN!

ALSO, VOLUME 6 WAS JAM-PACKED WITH MUSIC...

THANK YOU VERY MUCH...

...FOR PICKING UP VOLUME 6!

BY THE WAY, I'VE BEEN WONDERING...

IS THIS A CAT MANGA...

...OR A MUSIC MANGA?

THERE ARE LOTS OF SERIES ABOUT CATS...

...SO I THOUGHT IT WOULDN'T HURT...

...TO HAVE A CAT MANGA THAT WAS ABOUT BOTH MUSIC AND CATS!

SINCE THAT'S THE CASE, I DRAW BOTH OF THEM WITH CARE.

IT CAN BE BOTH!!

YEAH! SURE IT CAN!

I WONDERED IF IT SHOULDN'T JUST BE ABOUT FUKUMARU AND THE MAN'S HEARTWARMING DAYS TOGETHER.

I THOUGHT MAYBE I SHOULD EMPHASIZE THE "CAT MANGA" ASPECT MORE.

AT FIRST, I WAS CONFLICTED ABOUT IT.

APPARENTLY...

...I CAN'T DRAW PURELY HEARTWARMING STORIES.

BA BAM

...I WANTED TO LIGHTEN THEIR LOADS AS MUCH AS I COULD.

WHEN YOU CREATE CHARACTERS, THOUGH, THEY ACQUIRE HISTORIES.

WHEN I SAW THEIR BURDENS...

...SOMETHING FANTASTIC HAPPENED.

THANKS TO MY PROTAGONIST'S HARD WORK...

OH YEAH? WHAT'S THAT?

I WANT FUKUMARU TO EAT LOTS OF FOOD AND SLEEP, THOUGH.

SO YOU'RE ONLY HARD ON HUMANS, HUH, JELLYFISH?!

HEY, YOU'RE MAKING HIS LOAD HEAVIER!

WHILE YOU'RE AT IT, GO ON AND CARRY EVERYBODY!

I JUST KNOW YOU'LL OVERCOME THIS!

GO FOR IT, PROTAGONIST! YOU CAN DO IT!

A Man & His Cat

6

Story and Art by
Umi Sakurai

Translation: **Taylor Engel**
Lettering: **Lys Blakeslee**
Cover Design: **Tania Biswas**
Editor: **Tania Biswas**

A MAN AND HIS CAT Volume 6
© 2020 Umi Sakurai/SQUARE ENIX CO., LTD.
First published in Japan in 2020 by SQUARE ENIX CO., LTD.
English translation rights arranged with SQUARE ENIX CO., LTD.
and SQUARE ENIX, INC.
English translation © 2022 by SQUARE ENIX CO., LTD.

ISBN: 978-1-64609-138-6

Library of Congress Cataloging-in-Publication data
is on file with the publisher.

Printed in Canada
First printing, June 2022
10 9 8 7 6 5 4 3 2 1

SQUARE ENIX
M A N G A

www.square-enix-books.com

God that he will send unto us his holy Manifestations in their most perfect might, with the divine penetrative power of his Word, so that these heavenly ones may be distinguished above all other beings in every respect, in every attribute, just as the glorious sun is distinguished above all stars.

Although the stars are scintillating and brilliant, the sun is superior to them in luminous effulgence. Similarly these holy divine Manifestations are and must always be distinguished above all other beings in every attribute of glory and perfection, in order that it may be proven that the Manifestation is the true teacher and real trainer; that he is the Sun of Truth endowed with a supreme splendor and reflecting the beauty of God. Otherwise it is not possible for us to train one human individual and then after training him, believe in him and accept him as the holy Manifestation of divinity. The real Manifestation of God must be endowed with divine knowledge and not dependent upon learning acquired in schools. He must be the educator, not the educated; his standard intuition instead of tuition. He must be perfect and not imperfect, great and glorious instead of being weak and impotent. He must be wealthy in the riches of the spiritual world and not indigent. In a word, the holy divine Manifestation of God must be distinguished above all others of mankind in every aspect and qualification, in order that he may be able to effectively train the human body politic, eliminate the darkness enshrouding the human world, uplift humanity from a lower to a higher kingdom, be able through the penetrative power of his Word to promote and spread broadcast the beneficent message of universal peace among men, bring about the unification of mankind in religious belief through a manifest divine power, harmonize all sects and denominations and convert all nativities and nationalities into one nativity and fatherland.

It is our hope that the bounties of God will encompass us all, the gifts of the divine become manifest, the lights of the Sun of Truth illumine our eyes, inspire our hearts, convey to our souls cheerful glad-tidings of God, cause our thoughts to become lofty and our efforts to be productive of glorious results. In a word, it is our hope that we may attain to that which is the summit of human aspirations and wishes.

unjust; the Manifestations cause them to become just. Man is selfish; they sever him from self and desire. Man is haughty; they make him meek, humble and friendly. He is earthly; they make him heavenly. Men are material; the Manifestations transform them into semblance divine. They are immature children; the Manifestations develop them into maturity. Man is poor; they endow him with wealth. Man is base, treacherous and mean; the Manifestations of God uplift him into dignity, nobility and loftiness.

These holy Manifestations liberate the world of humanity from the imperfections which beset it and cause men to appear in the beauty of heavenly perfections. Were it not for the coming of these holy Manifestations of God all mankind would be found on the plane of the animal. They would remain darkened and ignorant like those who have been denied schooling and who never had a teacher or trainer. Undoubtedly such unfortunates will continue in their condition of need and deprivation.

If the mountains, hills and plains of the material world are left wild and uncultivated under the rule of nature, they will remain an unbroken wilderness; no fruitful tree to be found anywhere upon them. A true cultivator changes this forest and jungle into a garden, training its trees to bring forth fruit and causing flowers to grow in place of thorns and thistles. The holy Manifestations are the ideal gardeners of human souls, the divine cultivators of human hearts. The world of existence is but a jungle of disorder and confusion, a state of nature producing nothing but fruitless, useless trees. The ideal gardeners train these wild uncultivated human trees, cause them to become fruitful, water and cultivate them day by day so that they adorn the world of existence and continue to flourish in the utmost beauty.

Consequently we cannot say that the divine bounty has ceased, that the glory of divinity is exhausted or the Sun of Truth sunk into eternal sunset, into that darkness which is not followed by light, into that night which is not followed by a sunrise and dawn, into that death which is not followed by life, into that error which is not followed by truth. Is it conceivable that the Sun of Reality should sink into an eternal darkness? No! the sun was created in order that it may shed light upon the world and train all the kingdoms of existence. How then can the ideal Sun of Truth, the Word of God, set forever? For this would mean the cessation of the divine bounty, and the divine bounty by its very nature is continuous and ceaseless. Its sun is ever shining, its cloud is ever producing rain, its breezes are ever blowing, its bestowals are all-comprehending, its gifts are ever perfect. Consequently we must always anticipate, always be hopeful and pray to